S0-CID-583

Fact or Fiction?

| Faith Healing

Other Titles in the Fact or Fiction Series:

Fact or Fiction?

| Faith Healing

Miranda Marquit, Book Editor

GREENHAVEN PRESS

An imprint of Thomson Gale, a part of The Thomson Corporation

Detroit • New York • San Francisco • New Haven, Conn. • Waterville, Maine • London

Christine Nasso, *Publisher*
Elizabeth Des Chenes, *Managing Editor*

© 2006 Thomson Gale, a part of The Thomson Corporation.

Thomson and Star logo are trademarks and Gale and Greenhaven Press are registered trademarks used herein under license.

For more information, contact:
Greenhaven Press
27500 Drake Rd.
Farmington Hills, MI 48331-3535
Or you can visit our Internet site at http://www.gale.com

ALL RIGHTS RESERVED
No part of this work covered by the copyright hereon may be reproduced or used in any form or by any means—graphic, electronic, or mechanical, including photocopying, recording, taping, Web distribution, or information storage retrieval systems—without the written permission of the publisher.

Articles in Greenhaven Press anthologies are often edited for length to meet page requirements. In addition, original titles of these works are changed to clearly present the main thesis and to explicitly indicate the author's opinion. Every effort is made to ensure that Greenhaven Press accurately reflects the original intent of the authors. Every effort has been made to trace the owners of copyrighted material.

Cover photograph reproduced by permission of Royalty-Free/CORBIS.

LIBRARY OF CONGRESS CATALOGING-IN-PUBLICATION DATA

Faith healing / Miranda Marquit, book editor.
  p. cm. -- (Fact or fiction)
  Includes bibliographical references and index.
  ISBN-13: 978-07377-3507-9 (lib. :alk. paper)
  ISBN-10: 0-7377-3507-4 (lib. : alk. paper)
  1. Spiritual healing. 2. Healing--Religious aspects--Christianity. 3. Miracles. 4. Prayer--Christianity. I. Marquit, Miranda.
  BT732.5.F35 2007
  234'.131--dc22
                                                        2006022916

Printed in the United States of America
10 9 8 7 6 5 4 3 2 1

Contents

Foreword

> "There are more things in heaven and earth, Horatio, than are dreamt of in your philosophy."
>
> —William Shakespeare,
> Hamlet

> "Extraordinary claims require extraordinary evidence."
>
> —Carl Sagan,
> The Demon-Haunted World

Almost every one of us has experienced something that we thought seemed mysterious and unexplainable. For example, have you ever known that someone was going to call you just before the phone rang? Or perhaps you have had a dream about something that later came true. Some people think these occurrences are signs of the paranormal. Others explain them as merely coincidence.

As the examples above show, mysteries of the paranormal ("beyond the normal") are common. For example, most towns have at least one place where inhabitants believe ghosts live. People report seeing strange lights in the sky that they believe are the spaceships of visitors from other planets. And scientists have been working for decades to discover the truth about sightings of mysterious creatures like Bigfoot and the Loch Ness monster.

There are also mysteries of magic and miracles. The two often share a connection. Many forms of magical belief are tied to religious belief. For example, many of the rituals and beliefs of the voodoo religion are viewed by outsiders as magical practices. These include such things as the alleged Haitian voodoo practice of turning people into zombies (the walking dead).

There are mysteries of history—events and places that have been recorded in history but that we still have questions about today. For example, was the great King Arthur a real king or merely a legend? How, exactly, were the pyramids built? Historians continue to seek the answers to these questions.

Then, of course, there are mysteries of science. One such mystery is how humanity began. Although most scientists agree that it was through the long, slow process of evolution, not all scientists agree that indisputable proof has been found.

Subjects like these are fascinating, in part because we do not know the whole truth about them. They are mysteries. And they are controversial—people hold very strong and opposing views about them.

How we go about sifting through information on such topics is the subject of every book in the Greenhaven Press series Fact or Fiction? Each anthology includes articles that present the main ideas favoring and challenging a given topic. The editor collects such material from a variety of sources, including scientific research, eyewitness accounts, and government reports. In addition, a final chapter gives readers tools to analyze the articles they read. With these tools, readers can sift through the information presented in the articles by applying the methods of hypothetical reasoning. Examining these topics in this way adds a unique aspect to the Fact or Fiction? series. Hypothetical reasoning can be applied to any topic to allow a reader to become more analytical about the material he or she encounters. While such reasoning may not solve the mystery of who is right or who is wrong, it can help the reader separate valid from invalid evidence relating to all topics and can be especially helpful in analyzing material where people disagree.

Introduction

As a young man, Robert Peel became sick with the flu. It was a particularly contagious and uncomfortable strain. His friends were all ill, and he suffered from fever, pain, weakness, and inflammation. Peel's mother was a Christian Science practitioner, certified as a professional healer. While Peel's friends all went to the doctor, Peel stayed home in bed. His mother prayed with him—praying for healing that would help him recover from the flu.

According to Peel's personal account in his book *Spiritual Healing in a Scientific Age* (1987), after ten minutes of this "faith treatment" he was miraculously healed. While his friends lay sick for days, Peel recovered almost immediately, and was able to engage in his usual activities without ill effect. The difference between him and his friends, Peel explains, is obvious: his miraculous healing by faith allowed him access to a divine being capable of curing his disease faster than any mortal doctor.

Stories like Robert Peel's are quite common. Many people believe that faith has the power to heal. For thousands of years humans have looked to sources larger than themselves for healing. Members of nearly every religion and sect have some level of belief in the efficacy of faith healing. However, even though faith healing has widespread acceptance, there are skeptics.

Those who do not accept faith healing believe that the "cures" come about by natural processes, or even that more sinister forces are at work: frauds convince the unwitting that they are cured when they are still sick. In his book *The Faith Healers* (1989) James Randi exposes evangelical faith healers like Oral Roberts, W.V. Grant, and Peter Popoff who make millions of dollars from people who send them money, hoping to be "healed." Such cases, like those seen at faith healing events, are merely the result of the atmosphere and psychological factors, not actual healing, and lead people to believe they have been healed when they have not been.

Definition of Faith Healing

For those who believe in miraculous healings, a faith healing occurs when someone becomes well again through the aid of faith or one of its manifestations, such as prayer. This healing can be anything from finding that a cancer has inexplicably receded, that a depression has lifted, or that pain has abated. Faith healing applies to both physical and mental conditions. Faith healing can come about as the result of faith in a divine being, in a specific person or practitioner, or even as the result of faith in oneself.

For the most part, modern faith healing is associated with the Christian tradition. Christians look to the founder of their religion, Jesus Christ, for their healing. Accounts in the Bible have him healing many ailments, including blindness, lameness, deafness, and many more: "And Jesus went round the whole of Galilee . . . healing all manner of sickness, and all manner of disease among the people."[1] Faithful Christians call on Him to heal them of their own afflictions.

Faith Healing Outside the Christian Tradition

Whether Kalahari bushmen, Muslims, voodoo practitioners, or recipients of Reiki treatments, there are thousands all over the world who claim to have been miraculously healed or know someone else who was healed through divine intervention or by faith and knowledge in oneself.

Ayurvedic medicine is a system based on ideas found in the Hindu religion. It is becoming more widespread in Western culture. While this brand of healing does not require faith in a divine being, it is still considered faith healing because it is based upon principles taught in a religion. One of these principles is that being out of harmony with one's environment causes disease. In order to experience good health, the five elements of one's being must be in balance: "Balancing these elements in just the right way for each unique individual is the key to maintaining health and treating disease should it arise, whether it be physical, mental, or spiritual."[2]

Another form of non-Christian faith healing is shamanism. Shamanism is not itself a religion, but a description that encompasses many non-Christian religions that make use of rituals involving a feeling of ecstasy or that include out-of-body experiences. Like Ayurveda, healing in the shamanic tradition is thousands of years old. A specific priest, a shaman, performs a ritual that is said to aid in healing. For Native Americans in the Southwest, this may be creating a sand painting meant to take away the evil that caused the illness. Other shamanic rituals are common among voodoo practitioners, a variety of tribes in Africa, and some aboriginal peoples in Australia.

More modern forms of non-Christian faith healing are related to "New Age" practices, including forms of energy healing. While most of these practices claim basis in ancient Eastern medicine, many of the techniques and beliefs are of more recent invention, combining ancient and modern philosophies. One of the most popular of these techniques is Reiki, which asks that the person being healed have faith in her- or himself:

> If you are unwell, or have a problem of some sort, whether this is on a physical, mental, emotional, or spiritual plane, Reiki may be the key you discover that allows you to take responsibility for your own healing. When you first use Reiki, you open yourself to your own healing powers and become ready to accept the illness or the problem and understand its message.[3]

Secular Medicine

Secular medicine began to take a solid hold in Western society during and after the Black Plague's ravishing of Europe. This terrible illness depleted Europe's population and raised questions about faith-based medicine. People had previously turned to priests, but the onslaught of the disease had a secularizing effect on Europe's general population. Skepticism arose and placed distrust between the people and the priests, paving the way for the Enlightenment, which set the stage for the introduction of humanism and the study of science outside the context of religion.

Since the Enlightenment, medicine and faith have drifted apart. Many doctors today scoff at the idea that faith can affect a patient's health. In fact, many doctors insist that it does more harm than good. One of the most outspoken of such opponents is Richard Sloan, who acknowledges that faith is important in many lives, but should not be part of medical practice. He advocates a strict prohibition of physicians sharing religious activities, such as praying, with their patients:

> It sets up expectations between the patient and the physician that can be detrimental. It can be religiously manipulative or even coercive. If patients have religious concerns, physicians ought to do with those patients what they do with all other patients for whom they lack expertise—they should refer to specialists [i.e., hospital chaplains or other spiritual advisors].[4]

Others opposed to including faith in medicine cite instances of creating false hope in patients, as well as harm caused by the psychological consequences to the patient when he or she is not cured. Another problem many contesting the inclusion of faith in modern medical practice have is that some parents choose not to have their children treated by medical doctors. This can result in children's deaths, since children cannot seek their own medical treatment.

Movement to Reintroduce Faith in Medicine

Doctors like Harold Koenig believe that it is important to include a patient's faith in her or his medical care. Numerous studies have been done recently that indicate that faith and religion play an important role in health. In his book *The Handbook of Religion and Health* (2001), Koenig notes the positive effects of faith on health and refers readers to more than one thousand studies on the subject. While proponents of including faith in medicine cite these studies as proof that faith healing is a reality, many opponents dismiss the studies as poorly conducted and scientifically inadequate.

Some doctors advocate praying with patients, and probing them for religious beliefs. This is called taking a "spiritual history." Christina Puchalski is one of the doctors that helped develop the questions a doctor asks when taking a spiritual history. She has developed a course at George Washington University that helps medical students learn how to take effective spiritual histories.

Faith healing is one of the most divisive issues in modern medical practice. While most people agree that faith healing is not something that can be quantified exactly, those who believe in its efficacy feel that it works, even though doctors may not be able to explain why.

Notes

1. *The Holy Bible (containing the Old and New Testaments)*. The King James Version. Salt Lake City, Utah: The Church of Jesus Christ of Latter-day Saints, 1979, Mt. 4:23.
2. "Basic Principles of Ayurveda." The National Institute of Ayurvedic Medicine. http://niam.com/corp-web/whatishb.html.
3. Tanmaya Honervogt, *The Power of Reiki: An Ancient Hands-On Healing Technique*. New York: Henry Holt and Company, LLC, 1991, p. 38.
4. "Interview: Dr. Richard P. Sloan." Religion and Ethics Newsweekly, July 1, 2005. http://www.pbs.org/wnet/religionandethics/week844/interview2.html.

CHAPTER 1

Fact or Fiction?

Evidence for Faith Healing

Miraculous Healings Are Real

Reginald O. Crosley

Miraculous, or faith, healings can be explained by quantum science, argues Reginald O. Crosley in the following viewpoint. This line of thought is related to current physics theories such as superstring theory and chaos theory. Crosley does not dismiss practices that require a certain amount of faith, such as prayer and alternative medicine practices, including Native American and Asian traditional medicine. Instead, he contends that faith can heal by generating energy. In this excerpt from his book Alternative Medicines and Miracles: A Grand Unified Theory, *Crosley argues that faith healing, whether through Reiki, Hawaiian Huna, or Christian prayer is a very real way to experience miraculous healing.*

Crosley has a private medical practice and is a student of metaphysics.

In the annals of miracles, there are two types of miraculous healings. One can be called instantaneous healing. In a matter of seconds or minutes, the diseased organs or parts are transformed into healthy ones. The other kind of healing follows the same cascade of changes but the process of replacing diseased tissues by normal ones takes place over many days. Compared to conventional modern medicine, in either case, there is a great speeding of normal healing processes (Long, 190). The list is very long of vanishing cancers, straightening of deformed bones, restoration of sight and hearing.

[A Max] Long reported case, number twenty, tells how a [Hawaiian] Kahuna healed a broken bone instantly. A slightly intoxicated man fell and sustained a compound fracture of the left leg just above the ankle. A powerful woman Kahuna

Reginald O. Crosley, *Alternative Medicine and Miracles: A Grand Unified Theory.* Lanham, MD: University Press of America, 2004. Copyright © 2004 by University Press of America, Inc. All rights reserved. Reproduced by permission.

on location came upon the scene, kneeled beside the injured man and straightened the broken leg. Then she chanted a prayer for healing, followed shortly with silence. Then she moved her hands slightly over the leg. When she took them away, she said quietly "The healing is finished. Stand up. You can walk." The patient, now sober, rose to his feet and began to walk. The cure was perfect and complete. There was no evidence of deformation due to fracture (Long, 192).

In this case, the instantaneous healing did not come only as a result of a healing prayer. The officiating woman Kahuna was already a powerhouse of high voltage energy through her daily practices of rituals. Her own rituals are the equivalent of the meditations and long hours of prayer held by Christian mystics or healers. The Kahuna is already primed into a higher frequency state that will allow her to create the vortex of singularity and its coherent harmonic of virtualities. The healing prayer comes like the flipping of a switch to bring out the powerful amplitude of the high-self that actualizes a healing mutation or transformation. Here again, we stress the fact that there is no violation of the classical laws of physics but rather the introduction of the *principle of correspondence* by which the quantum set of laws and the curled up dimensions of reality are triggered to reorganize the quarks, the atoms, molecules, cells and tissues of the injured limb in a rapid manner because in that end of [the] spectrum of reality, things take place very fast in a fashion reminiscent of the first second of creation.

Miraculous Healings

One of the most spectacular cases of instant healing in the annals of the Western world, far away from the Kahuna lore, is the documented healing of the broken left leg of Pierre de Rudder, a laborer who worked in Jabbeke, in the Flemish part of Belgium. The healing occurred during his pilgrimage at Lourdes. While working with two other men to clear a fallen tree in 1868, the trunk fell on his leg and caused a compound fracture. Soon infection set in and a gangrenous wound developed at the opening of the fracture. There was also ulceration in the posterior aspect of the limb. As the condition worsened in the following weeks, a surgeon took out a bone fragment that left a three-centimeter gap between the ends of the fractured bone. After a year of suffering with pain, de Rudder could only ambulate with crutches. He did not want to have an amputation. When finally he got the opportunity to go to Lourdes in pilgrimage, various physicians examined him before his departure and the horrible deformity was witnessed and recorded. People who shared his railway compartment on the way to Lourdes were appalled by the odor (Harris, 343).

De Rudder had planned to walk three times around the Grotto as a penitential exercise but he could not realize this, thus he pleaded with Notre-Dame de Lourdes to allow him just to walk. But all of a sudden "he felt himself shaken, agitated, overwhelmed; he was beside himself, as it were" (Bertrin, 250). At this point, he was caught up into the vortex of singularity, the whirling motion of bio-energy field inherent to the location and heightened by the power of the collective or assembly. De Rudder then, without knowing how and why, got up and walked. He knelt in front of the Virgin's statue. His wife could not believe her eyes and sought confirmation of another companion, the Marquise de Courtebourne, who confirmed the extraordinary event. The purulent wounds had disappeared and the bones were in alignment, with the two legs returned to the same length, considering that a piece of bone was removed previously from the left leg leaving it shortened (Harris, 344).

That was an instant miraculous healing bypassing the natural history of medical cures, the lengthy Newtonian mode over many days or weeks, by switching to the mode of the complementary principle and the law of correspondence of quantum mechanics. Thus without a necessary violation of nature's own laws. This is another natural pathway to manipulate ordinary reality at the subatomic level without the expensive equipment of modern physics.

In the Kahuna world of Hawaii, there is another phenomenon that corresponds to the modality at work in spontaneous miraculous healing; this is the singularity of fire-walking. Long reported the case of Dr. William Tufts Brigham, a specialist in exobotany, curator of the Bishop Museum, "a great scientist, an authority in his chosen field, recognized and respected in the British Museum for the perfection of his studies and printed reports on them" (Long, 10). After witnessing three Kahunas of his acquaintance walking barefoot over hot lava at Kilauea, his curiosity was enflamed and he requested to do likewise under the protection of the Hawaiian mystics. His request was accepted and when the day came to venture into the ordeal, he was not too sure that he wanted to take the chance, as the memory of the infernal heat at Kilauea was not very encouraging. For the crossing they chose an area where the lava flows over a more level strip of about a half-mile wide. There was no turning back. But Dr. Brigham did not want to take any chances and decided to cross the lava flow with big boots. The Kahunas explained to him that keeping boots and socks on would be an insult to the goddess Pele, the entity that enters into [a] composite state with them to raise the protective shield against the intense heat. The deity did not agree to keep boots and socks from burning. The good doctor was adamantly opposed to that concession. Thus the Kahunas came up with an alternative. They offered the boots to Pele as a sacrifice, a holocaust of goodwill. They proceeded to tie *ti* leaves around their bare feet and grinned at each other as Dr. Brigham tied the leaves around his boots.

This done, the Kahunas began chanting in archaic Hawaiian, the sacred language handed down word-for-word for generations. The chanting of these words are a good induction of energizing the force forming the vortex of singularity. The chanting took only a few minutes and, out of courtesy, the Kahunas asked Dr. Brigham to go first. He declined the favor with the argument that age should go before beauty. Thus the oldest Kahuna went first, followed by the good doctor and the two other mystics came after. Without a glimmer of hesitation the oldest man stepped on the terribly hot lava. When he was nearly halfway, a distance of about one hundred and fifty feet, someone gave Dr. Brigham a shove who had no choice but to run straight ahead, running like a madman through unbelievable heat. His boots slowed him down as they began to burn with his first few steps. They curled and shrank, tightening on his feet. The seams were broken, causing one sole to go and the other began flapping at the heel. Finally, after what seemed to be a very long moment, he leaped off to safety on the other side. Upon examining his feet, he was relieved to see that there was not a single blister on them.

How does Dr. Brigham explain the bodily sensation as he went through the inferno? He had "the sensation of heat on his face and body but almost no sensation in [his] feet." There was a numbness in them. The Kahunas' feet were intact, although the ti leaves that were tied around their feet had burned away completely (Long, 35–37). The safety of these firewalkers was due to the emergence of the energy field that shielded them from incineration.

This is that same myriaforce responsible for instant healing. In the Old Testament book of Daniel, we have a similar account of the prophet's companions, namely Shadrach, Meshach and Abednego, being spared the searing heat of a fiery furnace. They had refused to bow down before a golden statue of the King's main deity in the plain of Dura in the province of Babylon, and by order of Nebuchadnezzar, they had been thrown alive into the furnace. The flames extended forty-nine cubits above the furnace. The heat was so beastly that it killed the Chaldean soldiers pushing the condemned men inside. Then the singularity occurred. An entity from the alternate reality of the Hebrews stepped in and contained the fiery flames and caused the inside of the furnace to feel like a dew-laden breeze. "The fire in no way touched them or caused them pain or harm" (Daniel 3:50). The entity was described "like a son of God" or angelic being. The radiance of his bio-energy field mutated the vibrational range of the flames into that of a calm breeze, and produced a protecting shield for the young men. . . .

Laying On of Hands

The Kahunas of Hawaii also practiced the laying on of hands within a modality called *Lomilomi* which is a combination of massage, bathing and deep manipulation accompanied by a psychic beaming of bio-psi energy to promote healing and the relief of pain (Long, 224). It is not necessary to reach the spiritual level of a Kahuna to perform Lomilomi successfully. Some herbalists or *docteur-feuille* ["leaf doctor"] (Haiti) have similar healing practices that include a bath with a decoction of several herbs or leaves. The officiating healer also recites a chant during the bathing, repeating that all illness was washed away and all pain was alleviated. The Hawaiian healer adds the power of words to the touch of healing hands and the touch of round stones raked from a fire and used to massage tight muscles and joints (Long, 225). At the end of the treatment, the practitioner places his hands on the hands of the patient and tells him to relax and let the healing energy run from his hands into him to produce a cure.

Up to the present time, my colleagues in academic or allopathic medicine and psychoanalysts use only the power of suggestion in placebo or in hypnosis. They do not acknowledge the existence of different levels and frequencies of energy fields and the capability of transferring radiant wave from themselves to the patient. Long has learned from the Huna tradition that it is very important to utilize a physical stimulus (a touch, a sound, a mandala, a vèvé or a pill) with a suggestion, a prayer and transfer of psychic force (Long, 233).

A counterpart of Lomilomi in America or the West today is *Reiki*, a derivative of the universal life force chi or Qi of specific frequency and spin and constituting the subtle self in the Tibetan understanding of the composite human being. . . . The Buddhist Chi is the equivalent of the Huna middle self, the African Semedo and the Afro-Haitian Gros-Bon-Ange. Reiki as an esoteric Tibetan Buddhist practice was rediscovered by a Japanese Zen monk, Mikao Usui, in the late nineteenth century and introduced to lay people in a formula that does not require years of study and meditation.

In the United States, one can become a certified "Reiki master" in less than a year. According to Tracy Cochran, a contributing editor of *New Age Journal*, one can receive initiation or "attunement" necessary to transmit Reiki radiant wave in a one-day workshop (Cochran, 60). That practice can reveal to the student or the novitiate the tangible existence of supersymmetric components in his or her person, "the sense of being accompanied by a higher power" that is nothing else than the awareness of being part of an unbroken wholeness of bio-energy fields raised to a high amplitude.

The fact is that this force can be passed to others either through a collective or through an Elijah-Elisha connection [i.e., from master to student] (Cochran, 60). As the Reiki master Wendy Lipson of Brooklyn explained, the tangibility of this force is such that blind faith is not necessary for it to work. We are hard-wired with those levels of energy and the attunement is "like plugging in the radio" (Cochran, 62). In the healing process, the modality consists in concentrating or focusing upon specific chakras for a specific result, the chakras being vortices of bio-energy radiance. . . .

For us, it is no longer a question of faith, auto-suggestion, brain washing or gullibility. We have been touched. Thus we know. For those who have not had such an experience, we advise an "openness" in facing the unusual and the paranormal. Skeptics even have a chance to experiment with the reality of those entities and their bio-energy fields in the context of the Houmfor, sweat lodge and some Christian gatherings. If the experimenters levitate, see heaven open or become immobilized by a powerful magnetic force in these settings, they will know without a doubt that simple imagination, suggestion and illusion cannot provide such phenomena.

Adepts and shamans and mystics of all the world religions know the sequence of events. Retrospectively, this is a large population of subjects that have gone through the vortex of singularity and its aftermath. Prospectively, the field is very open for contemporary intelligence to investigate with an open mind, without the corset of scientific reductionism. There must be a scientific explanation for these complementary phenomena besides illusion, ventriloquism and psychoanalytic theory; the answers most probably lie within the realm of relativity, quantum mechanics, superstring theory and chaos theory and other refined versions of these theories that will come in the future. Chaos theory in particular offers a cascade of equations pertaining to the sequence of changes occurring in a miraculous event and inside the vortex of miracle, the equivalences of relativity, the quantum fluctuation, the perpetual alternation of mass and energy, . . . contribute to the emergence of these eerie consequences that are the miraculous cures.

In modern science and technology, we have a wonderama of applications of scientific laws and principles but we still don't have the why. Brian Greene in *The Elegant Universe* asked why the string vibrates and Martin Rees the astronomer royal in his book *Just Six Numbers* asked why our universe exists in the first place, because from the uncanny appearance of the six numbers that constitute a recipe for our universe, the very existence of our world is "unlikely, very unlikely. Deeply, shockingly unlikely" (Lemley, 64).

Prayer Can Heal

Jeff Levin

This viewpoint is excerpted from Jeff Levin's book God, Faith, and Health: Exploring the Spirituality-Healing Connection. *In it, Levin addresses the effects that prayer and faith can have on the physical healing process. Levin focuses on distant healing, when persons pray for someone who is unwell and not in the same geographic location as the patient. In these cases, healing is transmitted through the prayers of the faithful.*

Jeff Levin has taught medical school and is a former epidemiologist. His research dates back to the 1980s, and it has helped develop the field of study that relates medicine and health to faith, religion, and spirituality.

Belief in the healing power of prayer is acknowledged within numerous spiritual traditions. These include established Western religions such as Roman Catholicism, mainline Protestantism, evangelical Christianity, and Judaism. Affirmation of the ability of prayer or focused intention to call forth a divine response for purposes of healing is also found within the writings of many esoteric or metaphysical orders, including Alice Bailey's Lucis Trust, the Theosophical Society, Rudolf Steiner's Anthroposophical Society, Max Freedom Long's Huna Research Associates, and Manly P. Hall's Philosophical Research Society. These traditions differ in their beliefs about what prayer is, how prayer works, when it is and is not answered, and why it can influence our health. But, according to Pierre Marinier, they all acknowledge that prayer, from the perspective of the pray-er, is a "means of access to the cosmic consciousness."

The possibility that prayer for others can promote health or healing can be studied. The conclusion that positive results

Jeff Levin, *God, Faith, and Health: Exploring the Spirituality-Healing Connection.* Hoboken, NJ: John Wiley & Sons, 2001. Copyright © 2001 by Jeff Levin. All rights reserved. This material is used by permission of John Wiley & Sons, Inc.

signify divine or supernatural intercession never can be proven by science. By definition, the concept of the supernatural implies something beyond or outside of the realm of nature. Scientific research requires observation of natural phenomena. Therefore, if there is a God that influences our health in ways that transcend all possible natural forces, no study can ever prove or disprove the fact. The best that we can do in relation to such works of grace is either to accept them on faith or reject their possibility.

This limitation has not prevented researchers from trying to document the healing efficacy of "absent" prayer, whereby pray-er and pray-ee are separated by space and time and do not come into physical contact. The results of their efforts, while empirically unable to prove divine intervention, are nonetheless provocative and challenging.

Can Absent Prayer Heal?

The most famous study of absent prayer, conducted by San Francisco cardiologist Dr. Randolph C. Byrd, was published in 1988 in the *Southern Medical Journal*. In this well-designed randomized, double-blind trial of 393 adult subjects, coronary care unit (CCU) patients who were prayed for by Christian prayer groups outside the hospital did better than patients who did not receive prayer. What made these findings so remarkable was that patients were randomly assigned to the treatment and control groups, neither patients nor hospital staff knew who was in which group, and patients and pray-ers never met. In essence, the study was equivalent to a tightly controlled pharmaceutical trial. This study has received a lot of publicity, and it is merited.

Intercessors were born-again Christians with an active daily devotional life and membership in a local church, either Protestant or Roman Catholic. Experimental subjects were assigned to from three to seven intercessors, who were given only their respective assignees' first name, diagnosis, and general condition. Treatment consisted of daily prayer until hospital discharge. All data were collected in blinded fashion. Results were uncanny. Prayed-for patients, in comparison with controls, had fewer cases of congestive heart failure, cardiopulmonary arrest, and pneumonia, and less need for diuretics, antibiotics, and intubation. These findings, according to Dr. Byrd, "suggest that intercessory prayer to the Judeo-Christian God has a beneficial therapeutic effect in patients admitted to a CCU."

A firestorm of criticism ensued. Subsequent issues of the *Southern Medical Journal* printed letters from physicians with heated comments about the Byrd study. One letter writer criticized the journal and its editor for attempting to return medicine to the "Dark Ages" by publishing this study. Quite the contrary, reasoned a follow-up correspondent, adding, "The *Journal* is to be encouraged in publishing such articles, because objective, scientific assessment of prayer, faith-healers, or what have you is an appropriate endeavor and one in which most readers will be interested."

I agree. Dr. Byrd is to be commended for tackling a controversial and provocative issue with great methodological skill and scientific objectivity. He practically single-handedly brought consideration of intercessory prayer to the forefront of research into body-mind healing and complementary and alternative medicine. This is what good science is all about.

Many other less-known studies of prayer and spiritual intercession have obtained similar results, and not just in humans. According to published reviews, notably the four-volume *Healing Research* by physician Dr. Daniel J. Benor, more than 150 experimental trials exist of the in vivo and in vitro effects of prayer and other spiritual interventions in enzymes, cells, fungi, yeasts, bacteria, seeds, plants, amoebas, and animals. Over half found that the intervention was effective—it healed, promoted health or growth, or prevented sickness or death of the organism. . . .

A study recently published in the *Western Journal of Medicine* by researchers at the California Pacific Medical Center addressed the limitations of earlier research. This double-blind, randomized, controlled trial investigated what it termed "distant healing" as a treatment in 40 volunteer AIDS patients with advanced cases of the disease. . . .

Results provide dramatic, clinically meaningful evidence of a healing effect of prayer in patients with a life-threatening chronic disease. . . .

What We Know About Prayer and Healing

This research underscores an observation commonly made by scientists working in this field. Successful absent prayer or distant spiritual intercession has effects on healing that have little to do with the religious background or ideology of the pray-er or healer. In reviewing this body of research for his best-selling book *Healing Words*, Dr. Larry Dossey came to the same conclusion: "Practically anyone's prayers appeared effective, regardless of their religious persuasion. This implied that no denomination or religion has a monopoly on prayer."

Despite these observations, there is a lot we still do not know about how prayer heals. I would second the conclusion of Dr. Michael E. McCullough, who reflected on the limitations of this field. Writing in the *Journal of Psychology and Theology* in a review of scientific studies of both intercessory prayer and prayer used as a coping device, he noted, "At this time, research on prayer and health is relatively primitive." Carefully controlled human investigations such as the Byrd and California Pacific studies are exceptions. But their results are useful guideposts, pointing to where we need to follow up. These studies offer confirmation that such phenomena are real. . . .

Much has been written lately in the press about research on prayer and healing, but the nuances of what these findings mean have gotten lost in the translation. This has resulted in

Volunteers guide a woman in prayer at the International Association of Healing Rooms, started by evangelist Cal Pierce in Spokane, WA. As of June 2006, there were approximately 460 healing room ministries in 26 nations where people could go for healing and prayer. Getty Images

distortions that promote overly simplistic images of God and the supernatural. It also has reinforced unrealistic expectations of how prayer might operate as a force for good in human affairs.

In 1997, I published my own take in the journal *Alternative Therapies.* In my article, "How Prayer Heals," I suggested several reasonable explanations for the positive results observed in studies of prayer and healing. Where these explanations differ from each other has to do with two key issues: first, the manner in which the healing effects of prayer operate or manifest in space and time; and second, the origin or source of healing in response to prayer.

How Healing Is Transmitted from Healer to Healee

A fundamental distinction can be made between healing that can, and healing that cannot, be explained by a universe that has what physicists call "local" characteristics. According to traditional, Newtonian physics, our universe is entirely local. That is, it consists of objects separated by space and time, and it operates according to certain mechanistic laws—for example, the inverse-square rule, whereby force dissipates as it distances itself from its origin. Space is three-dimensional and time is linear. In these terms, noncontact healing is understandable if we hypothesize, for example, that the healing effects of prayer are due to subtle energies that are transferred along a pathway from a pray-er who is physically near the pray-ee. But what about absent prayer?

Concepts of space and time as local present intractable problems for understanding the healing effects of absent prayer. No subtle energy yet identified has been shown to maintain its healing power over vast distances or times—not in a way that can account for the results of the Byrd or California Pacific studies. For these experiments to have worked, something else must have been taking place that was not caused by a physical energy as we know it and that violates the assumption that the universe is entirely local. The results of these experiments make sense, however, if the physical universe has "nonlocal" characteristics.

According to physicists, as I described in my *Alternative Therapies* article, "the statistical predictions of quantum mechanics are not fully explainable by the local universe believed in by most Western scientists and physicians, but instead require a nonlocal universe in which events or observations, regardless of their spatial separation, can be 'correlated,' or influence each other instantaneously."

The concept of nonlocality was first fleshed out by physicist Dr. David Bohm as he struggled to voice his dissatisfactions with quantum theory. He felt that the prevailing view of a universe fragmented into objects separated by space and time was false. He introduced to physics the idea that the physical universe is characterized by an intrinsic wholeness and interconnectedness. In *The Holographic Universe*, the late Michael Talbot explained the implications of Bohm's perspective for our understanding of space and place: "At the level of our everyday lives things have very specific locations, but Bohm's interpretation of quantum physics indicated that at the subquantum level, the level in which the quantum potential operated, location ceased to exist. All points in space became equal to all other points in space, and it was meaningless to speak of anything as being separate from anything else."

Theoretical and experimental work by physicists Dr. John S. Bell and Dr. Alain Aspect, among others, proves that nonlocality is not just a concept debated by scientists, but is real. Separateness of individual objects in space and time is apparently an illusion. This amounts to asserting "that there is no here and there or that here is identical to there." If that is true, as best-selling author Gary Zukav has noted, "then we live in a nonlocal universe . . . characterized by superluminal (faster than light) connections between apparently 'separate parts.'"

Nonlocal Mind and "Physics Envy"

While nonlocality is fast becoming old news to a generation of physicists, biomedical science has not yet caught on. This is ironic. Medicine, according to Dr. Larry Dossey, suffers acutely from what he termed "physics envy." In a review of his book *Beyond Illness*, I elaborated on his idea: "Dossey describes this as a reliance upon a reductionistic, materialistic approach apparently founded on hard science, on the atomistic truths of physics. The irony is that allopathic medicine is not even being true to its own envy; the physics to which it clings has been outdated for most of the twentieth century."

Dr. Dossey's great contribution has been his effort to reconcile medicine with new developments in physics, such as nonlocality. He is also responsible for extending discussion of nonlocality to matters of human consciousness. In *Recovering the Soul*, he introduced the concept of "nonlocal mind" —the idea that nonlocality is characteristic not just of the physical universe but of our minds. He described the implications:

> If the mind is nonlocal in space and time, our interaction with each other seems a foregone conclusion. Nonlocal minds are *merging* minds, since they are not "things" that can be walled off and confined to moments in time or point-positions in space.

> If nonlocal mind is a reality, the world becomes a place of interaction and connection, not one of isolation and disjunction.

The implications for our understanding of all sorts of unusual transpersonal phenomena—absent prayer, psychic abilities, healing at a distance, intuitive connections between twins and spouses—are obvious. Because of nonlocal mind, much of the hypothetically "superempirical" may really be empirical. So many phenomena may be perceived as controversial and unproved only because skeptical physicians, psychologists, and scientists have failed to acknowledge discoveries made by physicists decades ago.

In his classic book *The Roots of Consciousness*, researcher Dr. Jeffrey Mishlove has summed up the question nicely: "The confirmation of this principle of *nonlocality* suggests that psi phenomena, if they exist, need not be in conflict with the established laws of science."

In other words, the idea that prayer at a distance is capable of healing is not as far-out as one might imagine. At least it is not ruled out by any inherent laws of physics that render it impossible. If current views of physicists are taken into account, the therapeutic efficacy of healing prayer is both possible and probable.

Natural vs. Supernatural

As for the source of answered prayers, there are also two possibilities. Hypothetically, the healing response to petitionary prayer may originate from within nature—the observable physical universe—or partly or entirely from outside of nature. Explanations for the healing power of prayer based on the former assumption are what I have termed "naturalistic." Those based on the latter assumption I have called "supernatural."

Most prevailing explanations for how prayer heals are naturalistic. They do not imply or require the existence of God or a divine being who has supernatural characteristics— who is transcendent, or "located" at least in part outside of nature. Naturalistic explanations for how prayer heals are typically based on scientifically verifiable concepts—observable phenomena known to biology or physics. The "links in the chain" . . . for example—behavior, social relationships, emotions, beliefs, thoughts—are all naturalistic explanations for how religion affects health. Similar explanations have been proposed for the healing effects of prayer.

In a discussion in *Advances*, journal of the Fetzer Institute, I proposed naturalistic explanations for the results of many of the existing studies of prayer and healing. None of these hypothetical explanations invokes concepts that are particularly controversial. They are all decidedly exoteric.

> For example, experiencing the presence of a healer or healers may foster a sense of belonging or support, which research shows is healthful. Being the object of prayer or of laying on of hands or other ritualized activity may stimulate an endocrine or immune response facilitative of healing. The physical preparations for healing (for example, preliminary fasts, meditation, abstentions of one sort or another) may themselves be promotive of health. Finally, expectations of healing—regardless of the real efficacy of the healer, for esoteric or exoteric reasons—can lead to physical changes.

These explanations work fine, but only in certain circumstances. When pray-er and pray-ee are in close proximity or are the same person, or when the pray-ee is aware that others are praying, these possibilities offer the most parsimonious explanations for how prayer heals. But instances of absent healing, where the recipient of prayer is blinded from the intervention [i.e., is unaware of it], require something more. It is difficult to attribute results of the Byrd or California Pacific studies, for example, to the positive expectations of experimental subjects since those patients were not even aware that they *were* experimental subjects.

Several other explanations for the results of studies of absent prayer have also been proposed. . . . Commentators on the growing body of prayer and healing studies have invoked many unusual concepts as potential explanations, using terms such as "paraphysical" or "magnetic," "extended mind," "morphic fields," "nonlocal mind," "transpersonal," "psi," and "consciousness." To these I could add "subtle energies," "altered states," and other terms derived from parapsychology.

Such concepts are controversial. Some scientists believe that they are real; others are more skeptical. There is no consensus among scientists as to whether superempirical phenomena exist or are worth studying. But if they are real, they are intrinsically naturalistic. The fact that these phenomena may seem to "violate the tenets of prevailing biomedical conceptions of physical law," as I noted in *Alternative Therapies*, may be due more to our gaps in knowledge about the nature of the universe than to their transcendence of the laws of physics. Such laws, by definition, cannot be breached. Perhaps our current knowledge is limited. The laws of the universe that most of us learned in school have failed to keep up with the developments of modern physics, as noted in the discussion of nonlocality.

By contrast, an entirely different possibility exists for the reason that some people heal after they are prayed for by others: they are healed because God or a divine being that hears and responds to prayers chooses to heal them. Because such a being resides fully or partly in a realm that transcends, or is outside of, the natural universe that it created, its actions are termed "supernatural." As I have noted:

> While not a universal conception of the deity, such a perspective is a cornerstone of many of the world's faith traditions. Indeed, the possibility that there is a Creator-God who volitionally chooses to answer or not answer petitionary prayers by means which entirely transcend any naturalistic mechanism may be the most commonly held belief of people who use prayer or spiritual interventions for friends or loved ones who are ill.

This is not to say that God or a higher power cannot also heal through the natural laws of the universe. Many devout religious believers acknowledge the hand of God in "normal" healing, such as through the natural biological and psychological processes of the human body. Others see in healing by means of superempirical mechanisms, such as a subtle bioenergy, the presence of God's loving grace. After all, according to this perspective, these energies and forces were engineered by the Creator for salutary purposes. Notwithstanding these other possibilities, healing through supernatural intercession represents a category of explanation for the healing effects of prayer that, true or not, is distinct from naturalistic theories.

Science Confronts the Supernatural

This hypothetical explanation for why prayer heals cannot easily be accommodated by science, scientists, or scientific methods. As I have explained:

> The idea that there is such a Being as this who exists and operates outside of the natural universe—locally, nonlocally, or however—may be a challenging notion to rational scientists and physicians. Moreover, if such supernatural healing does occur, it cannot be "proved" by studies grounded in the

research methods of naturalistic science; it must be taken on faith. . . . [S]cientific methods based on observation of natural phenomena cannot be used to verify processes that are purported to exist, in principle, outside of nature.

Science, by definition, will never be able to prove the existence of supernatural healing. No research study that we could possibly ever conduct is capable of demonstrating that a partly or fully transcendent divine being responds positively to prayer by circumventing the natural laws that it created. But the same naturalistic research methods of science that cannot be used to prove the existence of the supernatural likewise cannot disprove it.

Faith Has a Positive Effect on Patients

Harold G. Koenig

Researchers since the 1980s have been increasingly interested in the correlation between religious faith and observance and the body's ability to fight physical and mental disease. Centers at Duke and Harvard universities are in the process of scientifically documenting the health benefits associated with faith. The following excerpt from the book The Healing Power of Faith *by Harold G. Koenig illustrates how patients overcome potentially damaging obstacles to their health through faith and what researchers today are doing to learn more about the faith-and-healing connection and to incorporate their findings into medicine today.*

Koenig is the codirector of the Center for Spirituality, Theology, and Health at Duke University. He has been involved in numerous studies demonstrating the positive effects faith has on health.

I met . . . a middle-aged man named Lee Daugherty* in November 1981, when I was a third-year medical student at the University of California at San Francisco. As part of my Internal Medicine rotation, I covered rounds at San Francisco General Hospital. Lee had been admitted on Halloween, suffering from severe complications of alcoholism. . . .

"You've had a terrible time, Lee," I said, consulting his chart, "and you're very sick. I'm recommending we keep you here as long as possible. You just can't go straight back to the street."

---

* I have rendered meetings with patients and other personal stories in a narrative form with the permission of those involved. When noted, I have changed people's names to protect their privacy.

Harold G. Koenig, *The Healing Power of Faith.* Touchstone Books, 2001. Copyright © 1999 by Dr. Harold G. Koenig and Malcolm McConnell. All rights reserved. Reproduced by permission of Simon & Schuster.

"I'll be okay once my legs get better, Doc," he said.

Even though I was as overworked as any medical student, I stayed with him a while longer. "You will *not* be okay, Lee," I said, placing my hand on his thin arm. "If you start drinking again, you'll be dead before summer." . . .

"I'll be all right," he insisted. "God has a purpose in my life."

His confident words surprised me. Lee Daugherty was one of the "lost souls" who can be found on inner-city streets across the country. Yet he seemed to firmly believe that God would intervene in his life. "How can you be so sure?" I was preoccupied with hard medical science, not the mysteries of faith.

"God has a plan for me," Lee repeated. "Last night, layin' there in the gutter, I saw kids in Halloween costumes going up Mission [Street], and I thought about my life. . . ."

He had virtually hit rock bottom the night before in that gutter. Yet now he seemed serene. "I think the Lord is showing me the way out of this mess," he said confidently.

"Maybe so," I agreed to keep his mood up. "But you're still going to need a place to stay when they discharge you. And you're going to have to go through detox again."

Lee nodded. "This time I'm going to make it, Doc."

You can appreciate my skepticism. Lee Daugherty had already been through half a dozen detoxification programs. He'd also tried Alcoholics Anonymous. He'd always gone back to drinking. Yet somehow he was convinced that the Lord would lift the burden of his disease. I suddenly recalled a passage from [founder of psychoanalysis] Sigmund Freud that had impressed me as a premed student. Religion, Freud had proclaimed, was the "universal obsessional neurosis of humanity." This undoubtedly hopeless alcoholic seemed gripped by just the type of delusion Freud had identified. *Well,* I thought, *at least Lee's faith brings him some comfort.*

I managed to keep him in the hospital for almost a week so that his withdrawal symptoms could be tempered by medication. And I helped find him a hotel room near the detox center. I also gave Lee my phone number and asked him to stay in touch, secretly fearful that I'd receive a call from a cop who'd found the number on Lee's lifeless body on the street.

Imagine my surprise when Lee called me that spring. "I'm getting married, Doc," he announced proudly. Lee had met Charlotte in the San Francisco General detox program. Like him, she had an abiding faith that God would free her of alcohol dependence. Together they were struggling through each day, determined to let their faith guide them to the inner healing necessary to break the grip of alcoholism. When I left California to begin my family medicine residency at the University of Missouri in Columbia, Lee and Charlotte Daugherty were sober and working, saving their money in hopes of buying a home.

"Congratulations," I told Lee.

"We couldn't have done it without God's help," Lee said, noting that they began and ended each day reading scripture. "I really like Ecclesiastes," he added. "'To every thing there is a season . . . a time to weep and a time to laugh. . . .' This is our time to get well."

Proud of my new M.D., with boundless confidence in the power of medical science, I attributed Lee's remission more to the techniques and medications of the detox counselors than to the healing power of his faith. But his experience had also sparked an ember of curiosity. Would he and Charlotte have managed to salvage their lives if they hadn't possessed such a deep faith?

A Lesson in Optimism: Ruby and Bill's Story

Ruby and Bill Clevenger were also patients who sharpened my interest in the health benefits of religious faith. During my family medicine residency in Missouri in the early 1980s, I often visited patients in their homes. The Clevengers lived in an old frame farmhouse in Callaway County. Bill Clevenger was eighty-one when we met. He had the strong, gnarled hands and weathered face of a man who'd worked hard his whole life, but he was now incapacitated by emphysema, and also suffered increasing deafness. Ruby, then near seventy, had a glow to her cheeks and a serenely cheerful manner. . . .

With his emphysema growing worse and threatening to make him housebound, and his deafness deepening his isolation, Bill Clevenger was a likely candidate for depression. But the handsome elderly man sitting across the parlor on the chintz-covered easy chair was obviously alert, beaming with friendly interest in my visit.

"Finally getting some nice spring weather," I commented.

Bill cupped his ear and leaned toward Ruby. "Ask him to please speak so that I can hear him," he said in a loud, toneless voice.

"Sorry," I said, speaking louder. I was prepared for Bill to slip into a sour lament about his failing health.

But he grinned warmly. "I like to talk if I can hear what people say." He explained that his hearing had deteriorated over many years, beginning when he was a youngster working with explosives on the railroad. "But I can still sing my hymns at church," Bill added.

"We're Baptists," Ruby interjected, "but we've gone to all kinds of different churches over the years."

There were religious pictures on the walls and end tables. They were standard, inexpensive pastel-tone prints—The Last Supper, Jesus alone in prayer, the Virgin and Baby Jesus. "I get them at rummage sales," Ruby said. "They always make me feel good." . . .

We were still looking at the pictures when the kitchen door opened and a slight, dark-haired girl of about ten entered, moving tentatively in the presence of a stranger.

"Cindy," Ruby said, taking the child's hand. "Say your hello to Dr. Koenig."

"Cindy's our daughter," Bill said proudly.

Cindy was mentally retarded. Ruby gently explained that they had adopted the girl after she had spent her first three years in their home as a foster child and it became obvious her disability would make adoption elsewhere very difficult.

"She's God's child," Ruby said with surprising conviction, taking Cindy onto her lap.

How many old people with their problems would have happily assumed such a responsibility?

Over the coming months, I often visited the Clevengers. Bill's physical condition did not improve. But both he and Ruby retained their uncomplaining cheerfulness. And they always made some reference to the role of religion in their lives.

Somehow I realized, *their faith is shielding them from depression.*

Soothing Fears: Edna's Story

As my residency continued, I became convinced that there were many people like the Daughertys and the Clevengers who used religious faith to cope with otherwise crushing problems.

I'll never forget Mrs. Edna Hanson (name changed), whom I met in the university hospital the day before she had surgery. Mrs. Hanson, a widow of seventy-five, was a ten-year breast cancer survivor who had later received a hip replacement. As sometimes happens, the artificial hip joint did not graft well. Now she faced the same painful surgery again.

That afternoon I found her sitting in a chair at the window of her hospital room, quietly reading the Bible.

"I hope I'm not intruding," I said.

She slid her bookmark into place and smiled. "You're not disturbing me at all," she said. "I was just reading [the Gospels of] Matthew and Luke."

After we discussed her physical therapy schedule, I became curious about her religious faith. Unlike other patients I'd encountered confronting major surgery with a questionable prognosis, she showed no obvious anxiety.

"How do you feel about tomorrow?" I asked. "It must be hard going through all this again."

She thought a moment. "Well, I got real angry when they said I'd have to come back for a new operation," she said with some embarrassment. "Then I got real sad, just sort of blue for a week or so. I lost my appetite and I cried at night when I couldn't sleep." She reached for her Bible. "Then I began reading my scripture. I like to say the Lord's Prayer out loud, just the way Jesus taught it to the disciples. It's calmed me down completely."

"You certainly look calm," I agreed.

"The Bible just brings me comfort," she said.

Indeed, her pulse rate and blood pressure were normal. Mrs. Hanson's case history stated that her husband of forty-six years had died three years earlier and her two grown children, who lived out of state, were unable to be with her. She was emotionally isolated as she faced the uncertainty of this new operation, yet coped with the stress amazingly well.

As I left the room, she switched on the table lamp and took up her Bible. The image of that elderly woman sitting alone with her scriptures remained with me on my rounds. Pre-op patients often required medication to calm them, but not Mrs. Hanson. Was she a rare case, or did her faith bring her both emotional and physical peace? Were Lee and Charlotte Daugherty and the Clevengers also exceptional?

What Medical School Didn't Teach Me

Nothing I'd been taught in four years of medical school or the first two years of my residency even hinted that religious faith could break the grip of addiction, shield people from depression, or calm them at times of emotional trauma. In fact, there were many examples in the medical literature that echoed Freud by implying religion was a neurotic crutch of little practical use at times of severe stress. In a 1960 report entitled "The Meaning of Religion to Older People," geriatric expert Dr. Nila Kirkpatrick Covalt had found no evidence to support the accepted belief that "people turn to religion as they grow older." As to the benefits of scriptural reading for the hospitalized patient, Covalt was almost scornful: "We physicians have learned that when a patient brings a Bible with him to the hospital and keeps it displayed, this action is a sign of anticipated trouble from an insecure individual."

Covalt described ignorant patients from "fringe" religious sects who brandished their Bibles and became so uncooperative that they upset hospital routine.

But the religious patients I had encountered certainly did not fit this pattern. Faith seemed to have brought the Daughertys, the Clevengers, and Mrs. Hanson a degree of protection from physical and emotional illness. I began to wonder if modern medicine, in its quest to shine the light of scientific truth on the last vestiges of medicine-show quackery, was ignoring the potential healing power of religious faith? . . .

The Center for the Study of Religion/ Spirituality and Health

Many of my colleagues tried to steer me away from what they saw as a marginal field of investigation. To them, the only demonstrable links between faith and health were the dubious practices of greedy television faith healers. I understood their concern. During my training in geriatric medicine, psychiatry, and geriatric psychiatry in the 1980s, I was flooded by discoveries on the frontiers of molecular biology and brain chemistry. Medicine could now chart the progress of cancers and cardiovascular disease from the cellular level and devise bold new treatments for these dread illnesses. CT [computerized tomography] scans and MRI [magnetic resonance imaging] technology opened exquisite windows into the living body. Whole new classes of psychoactive medications had burst on the scene, allowing us to treat previously intractable conditions such as schizophrenia and bipolar disorder. I was in the middle of a new renaissance in scientific medicine.

But I continued to meet patients like the Daughertys and the Clevengers whose health had been clearly bolstered by their religious faith. Explaining this phenomenon in scientific terms has become my life's work. Since my first tentative faith-health research, I have led or participated in scores of much larger and more thorough studies. Eighteen years have passed since I met Lee Daugherty. As head of Duke University's Center for the Study of Religion/Spirituality and Health, I've seen research on religion and health evolve from pioneering studies by Duke faculty in the 1960s. Over the years, our center's scientists have led over fifty major research projects on the relationship between faith and health. More than seventy data-based, peer-reviewed papers published in medical and scientific journals have resulted from these projects.

Duke's center divides the role of religion/spirituality in health into three categories: "Illness Prevention," "Illness Recovery," and "Treatment/Health Services Use." Other research facilities, including the Mind-Body Medical Institute of the Harvard Medical School and Boston's Deaconess Hospital, have investigated the physiological effects of spiritual practices such as meditation. But our center has focused on the impact of traditional religious faith and practice—including individual prayer and congregational worship among American Christians and Jews—on physical health and emotional well-being.

These investigations have rigorously followed the established techniques of medical and social scientific research. My colleagues and I have avoided the delicate issue of the supernatural. For example, we don't try to establish the validity of faith healing, but we do investigate the therapeutic or healing power of people's religious faith. We certainly do not try to prove which religious or spiritual beliefs are more valid or correct in an absolute sense. Despite our differing individual faiths, we are scientists concerned with concrete data, not evangelists dealing with theological matters.

Many of the Duke Center's studies have produced ground-breaking findings:

- People who regularly attend church, pray individually, and read the Bible have significantly lower diastolic blood pressure than the less religious. Those with the lowest blood pressure both attend church and pray or study the Bible often.

- People who attend church regularly are hospitalized much less often than people who never or rarely participate in religious services.

- People with strong religious faith are less likely to suffer depression from stressful life events, and if they do, they are more likely to recover from depression than those who are less religious.

- The deeper a person's religious faith, the less likely he or she is to be crippled by depression during and after hospitalization for physical illness.

- Religious people have healthier lifestyles. They tend to avoid alcohol and drug abuse, risky sexual behavior, and other unhealthy habits.

- Elderly people with a deep, personal ("intrinsic") religious faith have a stronger sense of well-being and life satisfaction than their less religious peers. This may be due in part to the stable marriages and strong families religious people tend to build.

- People with strong faith who suffer from physical illness have significantly better health outcomes than less religious people.

- People who attend religious services regularly have stronger immune systems than their less religious counterparts. We found that people who went to church regularly had significantly lower blood levels of interleukin-6 (IL-6), which rises with unrelieved chronic stress. High levels of IL-6 reflect a weakened immune system, which, in turn, increases the risk of infection, autoimmune disease, and certain cancers.

- Religious people live longer. A growing body of research shows that religious people are both physically healthier into later life and live longer than their nonreligious counterparts. Religious faith appears to protect the elderly from the two major afflictions of later life, cardiovascular disease and cancer. In this regard, religion may be as significant a protective factor as not smoking in terms of survival and longevity.

Hundreds of major studies by other researchers have produced similar findings. For example, religious hip-fracture patients recover faster than their nonreligious counterparts. Older people who attend religious services avoid disability significantly longer than their nonattending peers. After open-heart surgery, patients who find comfort in their religious faith are three times more likely to survive than nonreligious patients. The risk of dying from all causes is up to 35 percent lower for people who attend religious services once or more a week than for those who attend less frequently.

Faith Has a Role in Modern Medicine

Eve A. Wood, interviewed by Jeffrey Barg

Jeffrey Barg, editor and publisher of Physician's News Digest, *interviews Eve A. Wood about the role that faith has in health care today. Wood is part of a growing number of doctors who believe that incorporating patients' beliefs and faith into their medical treatment is important. Wood is also the author of the book* Mind and Meaning, *an analysis of modern health care and the role of belief in the healing process. In the interview, Barg and Wood address how physicians can approach the idea of faith and also the importance some patients place on having doctors who address their spiritual needs.*

P*hysician's News Digest (PND): What do you think is the proper role of religion and spirituality in health care?*

Eve A. Wood (EAW): There was a study done a few years ago through the National Institutes of Health looking at people's health care use. If I remember correctly, it surveyed 32,000 or 34,000 people—a very large sample of the American public. And they asked some questions about how people include complementary or alternative modalities in their health care. When you include prayer, over 70 percent reported that they used these modalities. If you take out prayer—prayer for self, having other people pray for you and so on—it becomes only about 30 percent. This is all faith-based practice. Most of them say it's in addition to what they do within the western medical model.

But most physicians are not asking their patients what they are doing in this area. So, the first thing is to develop an

Jeffrey Barg, "The Role of Religion and Spirituality in Medical Care," *Physician's News Digest*, February 2006. © 2006, Physician's News Digest, Inc. All rights reserved. Reproduced by permission.

awareness that this is going on, that this is a very important piece of people's sense of hope, guidance, comfort, what they're needing and what they're using to negotiate the complexity of what's going on. The first thing you've got to do is ask them. When I interview any patient or see them for the first time, I ask them, "Do you have a particular spiritual practice or faith tradition that is important to you?" Then I'll ask them what is their history with the faith tradition or spiritual practice. How is that relevant to their care now? Is it relevant in some way? How would you like me to include that? Do you have a place to talk about that? Would you like help in bringing someone in? Some people will say, "I'd like to talk to my preacher, pastor or the hospital chaplain." Some people will tell you that their faith tradition is negative for them at that time, that they're struggling with the belief that they got this because they did something bad and they need to talk about that with somebody. So, maybe they would need a psychiatric consultation or maybe a spiritual consultation. But for many people, their time of health crisis raises spiritual questions and issues. . . .

PND: If patients are already doing this in large numbers, why is it important for the physician to get involved?

EAW: If you ask most people: do they want their doctor to ask them, they will say yes. So that's one reason—because they feel that this is an important part of their care.

PND: Do you think that physicians need more training in dealing with this area to be effective or comfortable? And what would that training look like?

EAW: Yes. We can't teach what we don't know. And we can't provide support we don't fully understand. There are many different tools that have been developed on how to do a spiritual assessment. One of the most frequently used in medical training is one developed by a woman named Christina Puchalski and it's called FICA. It's very brief and it's used in a lot of medical schools to teach students how to begin to ask patients about their faith experiences. The American College of Physicians and the American Society of Internal Medicine have suggested the following four questions be asked a patient with a serious medical illness. Has faith, religion, or spirituality been important to you in this illness? Has faith been important to you in other times in your life? Do you have someone to talk to about religious matters? Would you like to explore religious matters with someone? You don't have to be particularly sophisticated religiously or spiritually to ask those kinds of questions. And then if the person says, "Yes, I would like to have somebody to talk to," to call the hospital chaplain or do whatever would need to be done to help make that connection.

Statistically, if you look at the degree of religious practices of physicians compared to any other profession, it's lower. So we're a little bit out of touch, in that sense, with the vast majority of people that might be coming to us for help. A number of years ago studies were done looking at various types of training. When you look at how many people who enter medical school believe in God compared to when they finish, the training drains out a certain percentage. And in psychiatry residency, if you look at that same question at the beginning and end of training, again that number goes down. A lot of the training not only doesn't teach how to include spirituality in medical care but in some way is teaching it out of certain people's experience.

PND: What do you think is the efficacy of spirituality in health care?

EAW: A lot of the regular practices that people engage in of a spiritual nature, whether it's going to church on a regular basis and praying, or some other things like regular meditative and yoga practices, have a lot of effects on human physiology.

They affect blood pressure, for example; they affect immune function, cardio and so on. In the field of mental health, people who regularly go to church are statistically less vulnerable to being depressed. When they get depressed, their symptoms are less severe and they recover faster. We aren't sophisticated enough to figure it all out yet. At least for some subset of people, engaging in some of these practices improves their health and even when it doesn't, they feel better. And my sense of myself, as a physician, is that it's my job to do what I can to make it better. What I can do to make it better isn't always about cure. Sometimes we can't cure. Like a person who has aggressive cancer—we're not going to cure that. But it's also about the doctor-patient relationship. It's about the quality of life. It's about the experience of that individual and their family and their loved ones and their friends going through that. And for the vast majority of people, aside from health benefits they may achieve through some regular spiritual or religious practice, there's a great deal of calm and ease that comes from that for themselves and for their family members. If you begin to think about the issues of loss in illness or death—family members become vulnerable also to all the ravages of depression and anxiety with loss. Having a framework of community and practice can help *them* heal.

The vast majority of cancer survivors will tell you that they believe that their attitude and their other practices had something to do with their recovery, even though we haven't been able to prove it. I believe that what we believe also affects what happens in our body, that whole notion of self-fulfilling prophecy. Not that it starts and stops there. I don't believe that. I think we have to do everything we know how to do in our practice, but what somebody believes—that they can get better or they can't—has some role in affecting whether they will or they won't. So, if there's some regular practice they can be involved with that's going to help with that, we want a person to do it.

Pentecostals Are Faith Healers

Allan Anderson

The following viewpoint gives an overview of Pentecostal faith healing and its significance throughout the Pentecostal movement. Allan Anderson explains the doctrine of healing as part of the atonement of Jesus Christ and the early beliefs held by Pentecostals that divine healing was the only authorized way to receive health care. Most Pentecostals today do not reject medical help. The author shares his own experience with his and his wife's own miraculous healings.

Anderson is a Pentecostal minister and the former principal of Tshwane Theological College in Soshanguve, South Africa. He is now a senior lecturer in Pentecostal studies at the University of Birmingham in England.

Most Pentecostals, charismatics and members of Pentecostal-like indigenous churches believe in divine healing (they usually prefer this term to "faith healing"),[1] and a few will even admit to their doubts concerning it.[2] Pentecostal belief in healing is often based on testimonies of people who have themselves experienced healing, and they see this as a direct intervening act of God. I share that perspective and offer a personal testimony to clarify my own presuppositions and set the stage for what follows.

In 1975, during a preaching tour in the mosquito-infested Shire River Valley in Malawi, I contracted cerebral malaria. I was unable to have medical attention for two days; I was delirious and felt as if I was dying. A Christian villager prayed for me until the fever broke. The next day I was well on the way to recovery and was preaching again within three days. A medical doctor confirmed from a blood test that I had indeed

Allan Anderson, "Pentecostal Approaches to Faith and Healing," *International Review of Mission*, vol. 91, October 2002, p. 523. Copyright 2002 World Council of Churches. Reproduced by permission.

contracted and recovered from the disease, but I had an injection of chloroquine, just in case!

What seemed like an even greater act of divine intervention occurred ten years later, when my wife Olwen and I were travelling in Zambia towards Malawi with a van and trailer. A partial head-on collision with a large truck resulted in us both being at death's door. I lost a lot of blood from external injuries. A Catholic priest gave me the rite of extreme unction and a Polish nun stayed at my side in the small mission hospital, holding my hand, and imparting incredible strength. The Australian doctor said that it would be "a miracle" if I were still alive the next morning. Lutheran nuns from Darmstadt [Germany] came to assist the Catholics. We were flown to hospital in South Africa by air ambulance. I was released from hospital within two weeks. Olwen, however, went into a coma after two days, which was to last for seven weeks. People all over the world prayed. I believe that I had received divine assurances that Olwen would recover. One afternoon, after she had been comatose for four weeks, the German healing evangelist Reinhard Bonnke (who lived in South Africa at that time) came to pray for her and rebuke the "spirit of death" that gripped her. She was in a deep coma with a "decerebral" response to stimuli. The neurologist had pronounced his opinion that she would not recover from her vegetative state. The next day, the nurse reported that she had smiled, and three weeks later she was beginning to talk. Everyone, the neurologist included, admitted that this was an event that had exceeded all expectations. Although Olwen's injuries were extensive and she remained in hospital for six months, we are now the parents of two children, our oldest born eighteen months after the accident that changed our lives. . . .

I relate these stories because the issues that are discussed here have profoundly affected me and are taken very seriously. God used a Catholic priest, Catholic and Lutheran nuns, medical professionals, a German evangelist; and the prayers of many people to bring about our healing. I will not pretend that everything has been perfect thereafter. Olwen and I continue to suffer physical consequences from our injuries, but we know that we are still alive because of God's miraculous intervention and answer to prayers. We know that God is compassionate and powerful, and can do anything in his love-filled purposes. Sometimes (but not always) these purposes are to heal and to relieve suffering and affliction. I pray for people to be healed even when I seldom see it happening, and I gladly receive prayer for healing when I need it. Sometimes it seems as if sickness overwhelms people, including my family and myself. But we Pentecostals remain convinced that healing is part of the continuing ministry of Christ on earth through the Holy Spirit. Healing, furthermore, is comprehensive and relates to all of life, not just the "physical" part of it.[3] This has been at the heart of the Pentecostal view of healing since its beginning. . . .

Faith Healing Is Fundamental to Pentecostalism

A fundamental presupposition of all Pentecostal theology is the central emphasis on the experience of the Holy Spirit. This experience includes [charismata] "gifts of the Spirit," especially healing, exorcism, speaking in tongues and prophesying. These charismata of the Spirit are, for Pentecostals, the proof that the gospel is true. In Pentecostalism, the "full gospel" is understood to contain good news for all of life's problems, and to be particularly relevant in those societies where disease is rife and access to adequate health care is a luxury. Without decrying the wonderful advances in medical science, I do not share the optimism of [Valparaiso University religion professor] Christoffer Grundmann that medical healing today is readily available "to a degree never before possible".[4] As [Reformed Church missionary] Claudia Wahrisch-Oblau has observed in China, the need for healings is in direct proportion to the unavailability of medical resources and the breakdown of the public health system there. Prayer for healing is "an act of desperation in circumstances where they see few alternative options."[5]

"Salvation," sometimes called "full salvation," is an all-embracing term in Pentecostalism, and usually means a sense of well-being evidenced in freedom from sickness, poverty and misfortune, as well as in deliverance from sin and evil. Healing from sickness and deliverance from evil powers are seen as part of the essence of the gospel, reference being made to Old Testament prophets, Christ himself and New Testament apostles who practised healing. In some African initiated churches, the healing offered to people relies upon various symbols, especially sprinkling by holy water, which is a sacrament providing ritual purification and protection. The symbolic healing practices are justified by the Bible, where Jesus used mud and spittle to heal a blind person, Peter used cloths to heal and Old Testament prophets used staffs, water, and various other symbols to perform healing and miracles.[6] In most other Pentecostal churches the emphasis is on the laying on of hands with prayer, sometimes with the addition of anointing with oil.

Early Pentecostals stressed that healing was part of the provision of Christ in his atonement, again following a theme that had emerged in the Holiness movement, based on such texts as Isaiah 53:4–5 and Matthew 8:16–17.[7] [Evangelical theology professor Donald W.] Dayton considers the "healing in the atonement" idea to emerge "largely as a radicalization of the Holiness doctrine of instantaneous sanctification in which the consequences of sin (i.e., disease) as well as sin itself are overcome in the Atonement and vanquished during this life."[8] British Pentecostal Harold Horton represented the vast majority of early Pentecostals who rejected "modern medicine." In his classic publication *The Gifts of the Spirit,* which first appeared in 1934, Horton speaks of "gifts" of healing "for the supernatural healing of diseases and infirmities without natural means of any sort."[9] He says that "divine healing" is the "only way" of healing open to believers and "authorized by the Scriptures."[10] Many Pentecostals and members of African initiated churches have rejected the use of any medicine, traditional and modern, because its use is viewed as evidence of "weak" faith.

The majority of people in the world today are underprivileged, state social benefits like health insurance are absent, and efficient medical facilities are scarce and expensive. Swedish bishop Bengt Sundkler, writing about Zionist churches in South Africa, said that people receive their healing message as a "gospel for the poor."[11] Wahrisch-Oblau found that prayers for the sick, and healing experiences were common to all the Chinese Protestant churches, and that healings were considered "normal" there.[12] Michael Bergunder shows the prominence of healing in the South Indian Pentecostal movement.[13] My own work has demonstrated the central role of healing in most African initiated churches.[14] That people believe themselves to be healed means that for them, the gospel is a potent remedy for their frequent experiences of affliction. The "full gospel" proclaimed by Pentecostals seeks to be relevant to life's totality and to proclaim biblical deliverance from the very real fear of evil. Whatever the source of them may be, evil, misfortune and affliction are the experiences of people everywhere, and Pentecostals endeavour to provide a solution to these compelling needs. This understanding of "salvation" has to do with deliverance from people's fearful experiences of evil forces that oppose their sense of safety and security. The methods used to receive this deliverance and the perceptions concerning the means of grace sometimes differ, but Pentecostals believe in an omnipotent and compassionate God who is concerned with all human troubles and willing to intervene to alleviate them. Bishops, pastors, prophets, ministers, evangelists and ordinary church members exercise the authority that they believe has been given them by the God of the Bible. Re-inforced by the power of the Spirit, they announce the good news of deliverance from sin, sickness and oppression, and from every conceivable form of evil, including social depriva-tion, unemployment, poverty and sorcery. The emphasis on experiencing the power of the Spirit is a common characteris-tic of Pentecostal theology, where the Holy Spirit is the agent of healing and deliverance. . . .

Faith and Healing in Pentecostalism Today

The "Third Wave" in evangelicalism was a term coined by Fuller Theological Seminary's Peter Wagner, following the two "waves" of the classical Pentecostal movement and the charis-matic movement [respectively]. Wagner identified the Third Wave with John Wimber (1934–1997), who taught a "Signs and Wonders" course at Fuller during the eighties and whose Vineyard Christian Fellowship spearheaded a new emphasis on renewal in the established churches throughout the English-speaking world. The Third Wave moved away from the idea of a "second blessing" experience of the Spirit to an emphasis on the gifts of the Spirit in evangelism and as part of normal Christian life. Wimber's influence on the charis-matic renewal in Britain was enormous. His first visit there in 1982 resulted in widespread acceptance of his message of "power evangelism" among older churches, especially in evan-gelical Anglicanism. The churches of Holy Trinity, Brompton in London and St Andrew's, Chorleywood became centres of the new renewal. Wimber's particular contribution was to demonstrate that healing is a ministry of the whole church and not just of a particularly gifted individual such as a heal-ing evangelist.

The question of healing in Pentecostal churches has been extensively debated, among others by British charismatics Ni-gel Wright and Andrew Walker, who both believe in healing but say that the claims about healing and the miraculous must be handled with care. Wright, with reference to Wimber, says that "the rhetoric about miraculous healing far exceeds the reality."[15] Walker reminds us that just as both dispensational fundamentalists and liberals . . . rejected the possibility of miracles, so those who accept their present reality will need to be very careful that "nothing short of total integrity in dealing with them will do." He says that believing in miracles "surely entails the moral imperative to protect them from fraudulence or from frivolity and shoddiness." This is ultimately a question of seeing the "miraculous" as holy.[16]

Pentecostals today, particularly in the Western world, generally have greatly modified views on faith and healing, compared to those of their predecessors. They frequently resort to modern medicine and accept the validity of "gradual" and "natural" healing. Rather than declare that divine healing is for all, most prefer, as [biblical scholar] Keith Warrington observes, "to allow for the possibility of healing rather than hold to an unconditionally promised gift of healing for all believers."[17] More credence is given to the idea that God sometimes chooses not to heal, and that suffering is part of the divine economy. More reflection on these and other issues has led to a more realistic and sensitive theology of healing, including a more nuanced view of "healing in the atonement."[18] Warrington also points out that the ministry of a healing evangelist has largely given way to that of a corporate healing ministry of the church.[19] This too is expressed in recent ecumenical consultations, where, the church is seen as a "community in healing."[20]

Healing and protection from evil are among the most prominent features of Pentecostalism that have affected its evangelism and church recruitment throughout the world. The central place given to healing is particularly relevant in the third world, where the presence of disease and evil affects the whole community and is not simply a private domain relegated to individual pastoral care. As [Harvard Divinity School professor and author] Harvey Cox observes in the African context, Pentecostals "provide a setting in which the African conviction that spirituality and healing belong together is dramatically enacted."[21] These communities were, to a large extent, health-orientated communities and, in their traditional religions, rituals for healing and protection are prominent. Pentecostals responded to what they experienced as a void left by rationalistic Western forms of Christianity which had unwittingly initiated what was tantamount to the destruction of ancient spiritual values. Pentecostals declared a message that reclaimed the biblical traditions of healing and protection from evil, demonstrated the practical effects of these traditions and, by so doing, became heralds of a Christianity that was more meaningful. Thus, Pentecostalism has gone a long way towards meeting physical, emotional and spiritual needs, by offering solutions to life's problems and ways to cope in a threatening and hostile world.[22]

Conclusions

All the widely differing Pentecostal movements have important common features. Far from being "the expression of escapist behaviour,"[23] they proclaim and celebrate a salvation that encompasses all of life's experiences and afflictions, and they offer an empowerment that provides a sense of dignity and a coping mechanism for life, and that motivates their messengers. Thousands of preachers have emphasized the manifestation of divine power through healing, prophecy, speaking in tongues and other Pentecostal phenomena. The message proclaimed by these charismatic preachers of receiving the power of the Spirit to meet human needs was welcome in societies where a lack of power was keenly felt on a daily basis. The main attraction of Pentecostalism in the third world is still the emphasis on healing. Preaching a message that promises solutions for present felt needs, Pentecostal preachers are heeded and their "full gospel" readily accepted.

Pentecostals confront old views by declaring what they are convinced is a more powerful protection against sorcery and a more effective healing from sickness than either the existing churches or the traditional rituals had offered. Healing, guidance, protection from evil, and success and prosperity are some of the practical benefits offered to faithful members of Pentecostal churches. Although Pentecostals do not have all the right answers or are to be emulated in all respects, the enormous and unparalleled contribution made by Pentecostals to alter the face of world Christianity must be acknowledged.

Notes

1. In this essay, *Pentecostal* will refer to Pentecostal, charismatic, and indigenous Pentecostal-like churches all over the world, unless the text makes clear that it refers to only one of these categories.
2. E.g., William W. Menzies and Robert P. Menzies, *Spirit and Power: Foundations of Pentecostal Experience*. Grand Rapids, MI: Zondervan, 2000, pp. 159–60.
3. John Wimber and Kevin Springer, *Power Healing*. New York: HarperCollins, 1991, p. 37.
4. Christoffer H. Grundmann, "Healing: A Challenge to Church and Theology," *International Review of Mission*, January/April 2001, pp. 29, 39.
5. Claudia Wahrisch-Oblau, "God Can Make Us Healthy Through and Through: On Prayers for the Sick and Healing Experiences in Christian Churches in China and African Immigrant Congregations in Germany," *International Review of Mission*, January/April 2001, pp. 94, 99.
6. Allan Anderson, *Zion and Pentecost: The Spirituality and Experience of Pentecostal and Zionist/Apostolic Churches in South Africa*, Tshwane: University of South Africa Press, 2000, pp. 137–41.
7. Donald Dayton, *Theological Roots of Pentacostalism*. Metuchen, NJ: Scarecrow, 1987, pp. 127–30. The doctrine of "healing in the atonement" has reappeared in a different (Anglican) form recently. See Morris Maddocks, *The Christian Healing Ministry*. London: SPCK, 1990, pp. 62–69.
8. Dayton, *Theological Roots of Pentacostalism*, p. 174.
9. Harold Horton, *The Gifts of the Spirit*, Tenth ed. Nottingham, UK: Assemblies of God, 1976, p. 99.
10. Horton, *The Gifts of the Spirits*, p. 101.
11. Bengt G.M. Sundkler, *Bantu Prophets in South Africa*. Oxford, UK: Oxford University Press, 1961, p.223.
12. Wahrisch-Oblau, "God Can Make Us Healthy Through and Through," pp. 87–88.
13. Michael Bergunder, "Miracle Healing and Exorcism: The South Indian Pentecostal Movement in the Context of Popular Hinduism," *International Review of Mission*, January/April 2001, pp. 103–12.
14. Allan Anderson, *African Reformation: African Initiated Christianity in the 20th Century*. Trenton, NJ: Africa World, 2001, pp. 233–34; Anderson, *Zion and Pentecost*, pp. 290–304.

Faith Healing

15. Nigel Wright, "The Theology and Methodology of 'Signs and Wonders,'" in *Charismatic Renewal: The Search for a Theology*, by T. Smail, A. Walker and N. Wright. London: SPCK, 1995, p. 76.
16. Andrew Walker, "Miracles, Strange Phenomena, and Holiness," in *Charismatic Renewal*, pp. 129–30.
17. Keith Warrington, "Healing and Exorcism: The Path to Wholeness," in *Pentecostal Perspectives*, ed. Keith Warrington. Carlisle, UK: Paternoster, 1998, p. 149.
18. Menzies and Menzies, *Spirit and Power*, pp. 159–68.
19. Warrington, "Healing and Exorcism," p. 151.
20. E. Anthony Allen, "What Is the Church's Healing Ministry? Biblical and Global Perspective," *International Review of Mission*, January/April 2001, p. 50.
21. Harvey Cox, *Fire from Heaven: The Rise of Pentecostal Spirituality and the Reshaping of Religion in the Twenty-First Century*. London: Cassell, 1996, p. 247.
22. Anderson, *Zion and Pentecost*, pp. 120–26.
23. Grundmann, "Healing," p. 29.

Fact or Fiction?

CHAPTER 2

Evidence Against Faith Healing

Healing Miracles Are Not Real

John A. Henderson

John A. Henderson points out in the following viewpoint the evidence against miracles and the problems associated with a belief in miracles. Henderson contends that failed miraculous healings can have negative emotional consequences when patients feel they are unworthy or do not have enough faith.

Henderson served as an Air Force flight surgeon in stations all over the world and is now semiretired.

Miracle as defined in Webster's dictionary is, "strange thing—to wonder at—wonderful—an event or action that apparently contradicts known scientific laws and is hence thought to be due to supernatural causes esp. to an act of God." Miracles, as commonly defined, are inexplicable or supernatural events and represent direct intervention of god in human affairs.

Jesus is credited with performing a number of miracles that are used to support the idea of his divinity. He raised the dead, healed people of various infirmities such as blindness and leprosy, cast out demons, walked on water, turned water into wine, and fed the multitudes. The power of performing miracles has also been exercised by others such as saints of the Catholic Church. Thanks to television and other media, we see and hear faith healers miraculously heal the lame who then throw away their crutches and walk triumphantly in front of thousands of wildly cheering believers.

Leprosy was a popular and visible target for miracle workers. It was hideous and scary to look at. People with leprosy were shunned because of fear that it was contagious. (It is only contagious with a long period of exposure to an infected

John A. Henderson, *Fear, Faith, Fact, Fantasy*. Boone, NC: Parkway Publishers, 2003. Copyright 2003 by John A. Henderson, M.D. All rights reserved. Reproduced by permission.

leper.) Jesus allegedly cured one leper. Thousands of lepers who existed before and after the time of Jesus were untouched by this single miracle. Finally, a miracle worker with the name of Hansen discovered the cause of leprosy, and man completed the miracle of controlling and curing the disease. Jesus' cure of one leper, even if true, was insignificant. Ironically, it is believed that the "Holy Crusaders" spread leprosy to Europe.

We have other types of miracles such as a person missing a flight and learning that the plane had crashed and he/she had escaped death. Another person who almost threw away a lottery ticket only to realize that it was a winning ticket. It was a miracle or god's intervention that the people in the incidents described above escaped death and won a fortune. For believers, it is not hard to see the hand of god in their lives or in the lives of others.

Most of us believe in miracles—we hope for a sudden twist of events so we can get a better job, buy a better home, or win a lottery. Miracles in that sense are simply wonderful, rare, fortuitous events. There is nothing wrong in hoping for miracles. On the other hand, rare, unexplained, terrible things also happen in a lifetime. In the phrase of statistics these are called chance events. But chance events occur in one's life whether one believes in god or not. To use rare and unexplained events as proof of a supernatural power, whether attributed to god or the devil, is unreasonable.

Negative Aspects of Miracles

The miracles of religion don't reflect favorably on god. For example, god's miracles show its capriciousness. If a terminal cancer patient gets well due to divine intervention, what does that say about those who die? Could it be that god doesn't love them? Why should an all-powerful and loving god choose only one person and leave out thousands of sufferers? Why not cure all of them? Why only one or two? What if a physician performs such miracles—randomly selects one patient and cures him, then tells all others to get lost? Would we think that physician is a good doctor or even a good person? If a human being walks on water or flies through air without the help of any mechanical devices, it means that god is bending the laws of nature to help that person. Why not let everybody else bend those laws and enjoy wonderful free-flying experiences?

In any case, religious miracles have certain characteristics. First, miracles are onetime, irreproducible events. Only the miracle-maker can perform that particular miracle and only at the time and place chosen by him. Nobody else, by definition, can repeat it. Second, objective and effective investigations by disinterested investigators are rarely allowed. Miracles are not subjected to peer review and evaluation. The very thought of asking for verification is a sure sign of lack of faith and is not tolerated. Third, miracles directly affect only a few people—the person who is raised from the dead, the person who is cured of his leprosy, or the person who is given sight or the power of hearing. Fourth, if a miracle fails to take place, it may be the fault of the person who is seeking the miracle. That person may have lacked complete faith in the miracle performer. The lack of faith may not be evident to anyone other than the miracle performer, but god, Jesus, angels, or saints know of that lack of faith and act accordingly. Fifth, the news about miracles is usually anecdotal; if something is written about them, it is usually long after the miracle has taken place. The truth of miracles and their occurrences is justified by the fact that so many people believe them. All of them couldn't be wrong, could they?

Life Should Not Be Run by Miracles

We cannot run our present-day life by means of miracles, whether they come from god, Jesus, or some other anointed and blessed person. Modern-day physicians routinely save the lives of thousands of people—not just one or two. They save the lives of people who come from all walks of life and from different economic and educational levels; people with different religious beliefs and no religious beliefs at all. It doesn't matter. If the physician has the appropriate know-how in treating, say, heart disease, most of his or her patients are treated and are likely to be helped. The skills acquired by physicians are subject to peer review. Techniques are adopted only when those skills are proven to be effective. Drugs, disease treatment methods, and medical equipment are documented so that all interested people can evaluate and verify them. Physicians pass on their experiences and learning through medical schools, internships, and residencies so that more physicians can learn the latest methods of treatment.

Modern-day physicians cure many diseases with treatments that could not have been imagined even a hundred years ago. Polio has almost disappeared. Heart disease is less of a threat now than it was in the early twentieth century. Mechanical devices such as eyeglasses and hearing aids enhance our sight and hearing. Contagious diseases that used to kill millions of people are now a distant memory. Prostheses and wheelchairs enable people to move about with comparative ease. Many cancers are being cured, more ameliorated. Parenthetically, if god doesn't want people to shorten their lives, perhaps god doesn't want people to lengthen them either.

Miracles Are Unnecessary

There really is no need to walk on water. If one is so inclined, there are thousands of models of boats one can purchase and enjoy the water sports. We can fly. We can pick up a phone and talk to people who are on the other side of the globe. We can turn the television on and hear the State of the Union message from the president as he is delivering it. Our agricultural scientists have improved the quality and output of our crops, which allows millions to escape hunger and famine.

Any virgin, if she is so inclined, can conceive a baby—it is now a routine laboratory event. Some scientists even claim that they now have the capability to clone dead people; anyone with enough money can have their pets cloned.

In other words, our life is full of miracles. If Jesus or any of his disciples were to come back to earth, they surely would think they were in heaven. The life we lead now was unimaginable and unattainable even to the richest and most powerful Roman emperors.

We frequently interact with saviors. Every day, we work with miracle performers who touch many more people than the ancient saints and saviors were ever able to do. Our modern miracle-performers, who are everyday physicians, surgeons, physicists, chemists, and engineers, do not claim to be the sons or daughters of god. They do not insist that we believe that they are born of virgin mothers, and they do not tell us that we are going to hell if we don't show obedience to them or their fathers.

In reality, most alleged miracles are card tricks. Careful scientific investigations usually uncover fraud, self-deception, or just plain mistaken interpretations of the events. Where there is skeptical inquiry, miracles cease. It does seem a little odd that most miracles delay that wonderful trip to heaven and eternal bliss. Even Jesus and Muhammad didn't seem to be in a hurry to get to heaven.

Conclusion

Jesus' miracles, as well as those of many of the saints are unimpressive when compared to the needs of mankind or when compared to the miracles of modern society. Turning water into wine at a wedding feast while millions of people die from starvation is a rather trivial miracle. Curing one person when thousands are allowed to suffer is not much of a feat. Saving one person from death while 240 others are killed in an airplane crash doesn't say much about the wonders of god. A run of the mill physician saves more lives in his lifetime than did many of the saints, angels, and gods. In addition, the physician doesn't demand that you believe in a certain dogma, creed, or god before he treats you. God and miracle workers should be concentrating on preventing global holocausts, nuclear winters, and the deaths of innocent people.

A miracle supersedes the law of nature—of god's law if you will—but there is no proof that any such miracle has ever occurred. Miracles occur in the minds of religious believers and are simply an attempt to convince themselves and others that their god exists.

A question we should ponder is why we continue to celebrate thousand-year-old miracles of dubious nature rather than noticing and appreciating our everyday miracles and savoring life to the fullest?

Studies Showing Healing
Through Prayer Are Flawed

Richard P. Sloan, Emilia Bagiella, and Tia Powell

Richard P. Sloan, Emilia Bagiella, and Tia Powell argue in the following viewpoint that many prayer and faith-healing studies are not conducted according to the scientific method and that many of the results are misleading. Additionally, the authors contend that even though many studies look convincing on the surface, one has only to go a little deeper to find real flaws.

Drs. Sloan, Bagiella, and Powell are colleagues at Columbia University in New York. All have written about the medical field and faith healing. Sloan's specialty is psychiatry, Bagiella's is biostatistics and controlled studies, and Powell's is psychiatry.

Even when studies are carefully conducted and show associations between religious activities and health outcomes, problems arise in interpretation of these findings. Thus, for example, well-conducted epidemiological studies showing that attendance at religious services was associated with reduced mortality (Hummer, Rogers, Nam, & Ellison, 1999; Oman & Reed, 1998) reflect only associations at the population level; they provide no evidence that making recommendations to patients to attend religious services actually will lead to increased attendance, let alone to better health (Sloan et al., 2000). Evidence from epidemiological studies must be confirmed by clinical trials before it can be converted into clinical recommendations.

One common problem with observational studies such as the ones often reported in this literature is that individuals assign themselves to the risk category. This phenomenon can

Richard P. Sloan, Emilia Bagiella, and Tia Powell, *Faith and Health*. New York: Guilford Press, 2001. © 2001 The Guilford Press, a division of Guilford Publications, Inc. All rights reserved. Reproduced by permission.

lead to biased associations resulting from self-selection. Individuals choose to attend religious services; they are not assigned randomly to attend. This self-selection may represent a prototype of risk factors, that is, attending religious services may be only one of several related factors that predispose people or to protect them from specific events. This possibility cannot be dismissed without a trial in which participants are assigned at random to different experimental conditions.

Although epidemiological results generally are confirmed by clinical trials, this is not always the case. For example, recent results from randomized clinical trials suggest that, contrary to the evidence from epidemiological studies, a low-fat, high-fiber diet does not protect from colorectal cancer (Alberts et al., 2000; Schatzkin et al., 2000). Only a clinical trial, in which patients are randomly assigned either to receive or not receive a recommendation to attend religious services, could help to determine whether such a recommendation will lead to increased church attendance and ultimately to better health. Because there are likely to be significant differences between the health effects of attending religious services on one's own and those of attending because one's physician recommends it, a trial such as this would be problematic, difficult to conduct, and yield meaningless results. . . .

Another illustration of bad science is provided by a . . . paper from [Codirector of the Center for Spirituality, Theology, and Health Harold G.] Koenig's group (Helm, Hays, Flint, Koenig, & Blazer, 2000) that examined associations between private religious behavior (e.g., prayer, reading the Bible) and mortality. In the overall analysis, they found no association. However, after dichotomizing participants by functional status (those with and those without impairments), the authors reported that among the unimpaired, private religious behavior was associated with a significant survival advantage, even after control for relevant confounders. They justify this analytic strategy by suggesting that "praying in a foxhole", that is, offering prayers when already impaired and presumably in times of need at the end of life, may be different from a "long-term habit of private devotionals" (p. M402). This represents breathtaking post hoc hypothesizing. First, it is axiomatic that in survival analyses, variables known to influence survival, for example, functional status, are entered prior to variables under investigation, in this case private religious behavior. When in the overall analysis, the authors followed this approach, they found no effect of religious behavior, and this is where the analysis should have ended. Second, how do the authors know that those with impairments do not have a lifetime history of private devotionals? Third, and most important, the authors' strategy violates all standards of scientific methodology: Cutting the sample into enough pieces and analyzing each one separately eventually will produce a significant *p* value [a statistical value indicating probabilities in testing] by chance alone. Why stop with functional status? Why not look separately at men and women, blacks and whites, younger versus older elderly, those living alone versus those living with others? This simply is bad science.

With physicians increasingly called on to practice evidence-based medicine, it simply is unacceptable to recommend practices whose efficacy has not been demonstrated and that, as we indicate in the next section, raise substantial ethical concerns. The argument that the empirical literature justifies engaging in religious activity as adjunctive medical treatments is unsupported.

Ethical Issues

In addition to questions about the empirical studies of purported relationships between religious activity and health outcomes, there are significant ethical concerns. Here we address four such concerns: coercion, privacy, doing harm, and discrimination.

Coercion. Health professionals, even in these days of consumer advocacy, retain influence over their patients by virtue of their medical expertise. When doctors depart from areas of established expertise to promote a nonmedical agenda, they abuse their status as professionals. Thus we question making inquiries into the patient's spiritual life in the service of making recommendations that link religious practice with better health outcomes. In *The Healing Power of Faith*, Koenig (1999) provides recommendations to enhance the health of those who are not religious (pp. 280–281):

- Consider attending a church or synagogue.

- Consider reading religious scriptures.

- Try to emulate the behavior of truly religious/spiritual persons at your place of work. He even provides advice for patients who already are religious (pp. 277–278):

- Consider attending services more frequently.

- Attend a prayer or Scripture study group weekly.

- Get up 30 minutes earlier and spend that time in prayer.

- Take a few minutes each day to pray with your family.

Advice such as this may be perfectly appropriate from the clergy, but in the context of a physician-patient interaction, it is inappropriate and potentially coercive. Do we really want physicians dispensing advice about our religious lives? And if doctors are to make coercive recommendations to patients, should they not select those interventions with the greatest likelihood of benefit? Because more than one-half of Americans are obese and approximately 25% still smoke, a conscientious doctor ought to address these problems before asking a patient to spend that time in prayer. Particularly in this era of 8-minute patient visits, any minute of discussion on one subject, such as religion, means not discussing something else, such as hypertension. Any recommendation to do one thing, such as pray, decreases the likelihood of a patient following another recommendation, such as smoking cessation or dieting. Thus, when doctors take on the work of the clergy, they become both bad clergy and bad doctors.

Privacy. A second ethical consideration involves the limits of medical intervention. For many patients, religious pursuits are a private matter, even if the evidence were to show a solid link between religious activity and health. Socioeconomic status and marital status, for example, are associated with health outcomes (Adler et al., 1994; Ebrahim, Wannamethee, McCallum, Walker, & Shaper, 1995), but physicians do not dispense advice that presumes to enhance them. Evidence also suggests that for women, early rather than late childbearing may reduce the risk of various cancers (Lambe, Thorn, Sparen, Bergstrom, & Adami, 1996; Ramon et al., 1996), but we would recoil at a physician recommending to a young woman, either married or single, that she have a child to reduce this risk. These matters are personal and private, even if they are related to health. Many patients regard their religious faith as even more personal and private.

Doing Harm. A third ethical problem concerns the possibility of actually doing harm. Linking religious activities and better health outcomes can be actively harmful to patients, who already must confront age-old folk wisdom that illness is due to their own moral failure (Gould, 1981; Groopman, 2000). Within any individual religion, are the more devout adherents "better" people, more deserving of health than others? If evidence showed health advantages of some religious denominations over others, should physicians be guided by this evidence to counsel conversion? Attempts to link religious and spiritual activities to health are reminiscent of the now discredited research suggesting that different ethnic groups show differing levels of moral probity, intelligence, or other measures of social worth (Gould, 1981). Because all humans, devout or profane, ultimately will succumb to illness, we wish to avoid the additional burden of guilt for moral failure for those whose physical health fails before our own.

Discrimination. A fourth ethical concern is discrimination. Proponents of making religious activity an adjunctive medical treatment assert that there is substantial evidence that religious activity is associated with beneficial health outcomes. "We have recently completed a systematic review of over 1200 studies on the religion/health relationship. . . . The vast majority of these studies show a relationship between greater religious involvement and better mental health, better physical health, or lower use of health services" (Koenig, Idler, et al., 1999, p. 124). These same proponents recommend that physicians probe patients' spiritual history to determine if religion and spirituality are important in treating their medical condition. Matthews et al. (1998) recommend that clinicians ask, "What can I do to support your faith or religious commitment?" to patients who respond favorably to questions about whether religion or faith are "helpful in handling your illnes" (p. 123). Thus recommendations to encourage religious activity are to be made only to those patients who affirm their importance and not to those who do not. This creates an interesting and difficult ethical dilemma: Given their assertion of the overwhelming evidence that religious activity confers health benefits, how can they in good conscience withhold this recommendation from patients for whom religion is not important? This is like determining patients' views on antibiotics before recommending them to treat pneumonia. It creates two classes of patients: one for whom an effective and life-extending treatment is recommended and another for whom it is not. To do this surely is unethical, given the purported strength of the evidence. Their hesitation suggests that these health practitioners do not really believe their own recommendations are based in fact. They know they have strayed into the problematic area of individual choice and personal values. Suspecting that the weight of medical science fails to support them, they cannot make their recommendations with a clear conscience.

Conclusions

Serious methodological and empirical issues continue to plague the literature on religion and health. Even well-conducted studies demonstrate only a weak or nonexistent association, and these associations exist only at the epidemiological level. Without compelling evidence from intervention studies to demonstrate that promoting religious activity actually leads to improved health outcomes, no empirical basis exists for making religious activity adjunctive medical treatments.

Beyond the empirical literature, there are important ethical concerns surounding associations between religion and health that have barely been addressed, let alone resolved. In a country of growing religious heterogeneity the possibility of serious ethical conflicts from unwarranted medical intrusions into religious life is real.

These conclusions are relevant to the issue of bringing religious activity into medical practice. Concerns of patients about religion and health are best addressed by clergy, to whom referrals can readily be made. Professional clergy, whether they are health care chaplains or not, do not have conflicting roles in these matters, as physicians do. They are not bound by the limits of science. Neither are their relationships with patients troubled by role asymmetry with regard to health. Matters of religion and health may indeed be important to patients, but they are not the business of doctors.

References
1. N.E. Adler et al., "Socioeconomic Status and Health: The Challenge of the Gradient," *American Psychologist*, no. 49, 1994.

2. D.S. Alberts et al., "Lack of Effect of a High-Fiber Cereal Supplement on the Recurrence of Colorectal Adenomas," *New England Journal of Medicine*, no. 342, 2000.
3. S.J. Gould, *The Mismeasure of Man*. New York: Norton, 1981.
4. J. Groopman, "Your Cancer Isn't Your Fault," *New York Times*, April 21, 2000.
5. H.M. Helm et al., "Does Private Religion Activity Prolong Survival? A Six-Year Follow-Up Study of 3,851 Older Adults," *Journal of Gerontology*, no. 55A, 2000.
6. R.A. Hummer et al., "Religious Involvement and U.S. Adult Mortality," *Demography*, no. 36, 1999.
7. H.G. Koenig, *The Healing Power of Faith*. New York: Simon & Schuster, 1999.
8. H.G. Koenig et al., "Religion, Spirituality, and Medicine: A Rebuttal to Skeptics," *International Journal of Psychiatry in Medicine*, no. 19, 1999.
9. M. Lambe et al., "Malignant Melanoma: Reduced Risk Associated with Early Childbearing and Multiparity," *Melanoma Research*, no. 6, 1996.
10. D.A. Matthews et al., "Religious Commitment and Health Status," *Archives of Family Medicine*, no. 7, 1998.
11. D. Oman and D. Reed, "Religion and Mortality Among the Community-Dwelling Elderly," *American Journal of Public Health*, no. 88, 1998.
12. J.M. Ramon et al., "Age at First Full-Term Pregnancy, Lactation and Parity and Risk of Breast Cancer: A Case-Control Study in Spain," *European Journal of Epidemiology*, no. 12, 1996.
13. A. Schatzkin et al., "Lack of Effect of a Low-Fat, High-Fiber Diet on the Recurrence of Colorectal Adenomas," *New England Journal of Medicine*, no. 342, 2000.
14. R. Sloan, E. Bagiella, and T. Powell, "Religion, Spirituality, and Medicine," *Lancet*, no. 353, 1999.

Reliance on Faith Healing Can Harm Patients

Bruce L. Flamm

Opponents of a movement to reintroduce elements of faith into medical treatment worry about the effect of encouraging faith-healing practices. In the following viewpoint, Bruce L. Flamm, a clinical medicine professor in the Department of Obstetrics and Gynecology at the University of California–Irvine Medical Center, asserts that incorporating faith into medicine harms patients more than it helps them. Flamm contends that patients' emotional, mental, and physical health are adversely affected when emphasis is placed on faith healing.

It is often claimed that faith healing may not work but at least does no harm. However, as will be demonstrated in this article, reliance on faith healing can indirectly cause serious harm and even death. Therefore, there is an inherent danger in the publication of studies that advocate healing by faith. Nevertheless, dozens of studies claiming to have confirmed some therapeutic value of distant prayer and other "distant healing" methods have recently appeared in the medical literature. Although faith healing has been advocated by religious groups for millennia, the issue here is the propriety of making supernatural claims in medical journals. It is one thing to tell an audience at a religious revival that prayers yield miracle cures, but it is quite another thing to make the same such claims in a scientific journal.

This article [uses] . . . the Cha et al. faith-healing study[1] as a model to demonstrate the problems that arise when faith-based studies are published in medical journals. The first article investigated methodological flaws in faith based studies

Bruce L. Flamm, "Inherent Dangers of Faith-Healing Studies," *The Scientific Review of Alternative Medicine*, vol. 8, no. 2, Fall-Winter 2004–05. Reproduced by permission.

while the second article focused on paradoxical questions that arise in such publications.[2,3] This third article will evaluate several of the dangers inherent in the Cha study and all similar publications.

1. Faith healing can cause patients to shun effective medical care. This is perhaps the greatest danger of any study that touts the efficacy of faith healing. In the Cha study, prayer appeared to double the in vitro fertilization (IVF) success rate. Since any method that can increase the success rate of IVF by even a few percent would be hailed as a major achievement, these results were astounding. The news media were quick to disseminate this seemingly favorable information to the public.[4-6] The apparent effects of prayer were so dramatic that it would not take a "leap of faith" for infertile women to conclude that prayer is more effective than medical intervention as a cure for infertility. This conclusion could cause some women to forgo medical care and thus miss out on the proven benefits of modern infertility treatments. In other specialties the consequences of avoiding medical care because of reliance on religious rituals and faith healing have been well documented.[7] A recent study identified 158 children who died due to reliance on faith healing and religion-motivated medical neglect.[8]

2. Doctors who accept faith-healing study results might diminish their medical efforts. Doctors as well as patients might change attitudes and practices in response to faith-healing studies published in medical journals. Why worry about proper clinical techniques and strict laboratory protocols that could at best potentially increase pregnancy success rates by a few percentage points when prayer is easy and far more efficacious? This may seem ridiculous, but if the Cha study results are to be taken seriously, it is not illogical. On the other hand, if the Cha study results are not to be taken seriously, why were they published in a peer-reviewed, scientific medical journal?

3. Faith-healing studies could steer third-party payers toward faith-based interventions. In the United States each IVF treatment cycle costs an average of $9,000, and several cycles are often required to achieve a viable pregnancy. For patients who require IVF, the cost of each live birth has been estimated at over more than $50,000.[9] Since IVF is costly for health insurance companies, if the Cha study results were valid, it would be logical for these organizations to advocate the introduction of prayer into infertility programs. The claimed doubling of IVF success rates could save insurance companies an average of $25,000 per patient. With millions of dollars at stake and with these compelling study results as evidence, insurance companies could insist that prayer be tried first.

4. Faith-healing studies raise informed-consent issues. The Cha study was conducted without informed consent. This is unethical, potentially dangerous, and possibly illegal. Placebo effect could have been avoided by first properly informing patients about the study and then, with their permission, blinding them to which group they were assigned. Lack of consent perhaps explains why none of the prayer recipients was located in the United States. Nevertheless, it is doubtful that the institutional review board of any university in the United States would waive the informed-consent requirement simply because the patients to be experimented upon lived outside of the United States.

Using patients as research subjects without informed consent also violates both the Nuremberg Code and the Helsinki Declaration. Furthermore, it is not logical to claim that informed consent was unnecessary because the intervention was only prayer and then to claim that the same innocuous intervention actually had profound physical effects on study patients. This is especially true since numerous claims made in previously published papers by one of the study's authors indicate that at least some of the people involved with this study believed, from the project's inception, that the intervention

could have very real effects on uninformed human subjects.⁰
Furthermore, because the study was conducted in Korea, where
the majority of the population is Buddhist, Shamanist, or
nonreligious, many study patients might have objected to
Christian prayers as unwanted, blasphemous, or antithetical to
their personal beliefs. But since the study was conducted without their knowledge or permission, the study subjects had no
way to voice their objections or to opt out of the study. . . .

5. Faith-healing studies raise patient confidentiality issues. In
the Cha study, photographs of the study patients were obtained and circulated all over the world without the patients'
knowledge or permission. Infertility is a personal issue for
many women and circulation of their photos by fax and mail
to strangers could cause emotional distress. Faith-healing researchers would be well advised to become familiar with the
Health Insurance Portability and Accountability Act of 1996
(HIPAA) and the penalties for violating this federal law.

6. Faith healing promotes guilt. Many infertility patients believe that they are being punished by God for some "sin" that
they may have previously committed. The implication that
prayer can increase fertility would reinforce this belief. It
could also undermine people's religious identity. Couples of
other faiths who believe the study's results might conclude
that their only hope of having a child would be to abandon
their own faith and convert to Christianity. While this might
be seen as a victory for the prayer-group participants in the
Cha study, the converts would have been won under false pre-
tenses if the study results were not valid and reproducible.

*7. Faith-healing studies encourage acceptance of magical and
irrational thinking.* The Cha study implies that some type of
supernatural power had an effect on many of the study patients. Some readers might believe that God or some other deity was at work, while other readers might assume that some

type of paranormal, psychic, or otherwise magical power worked without the need for a deity. In any case, something beyond the laws of physics is presumed to have occurred in this study. If the editors and reviewers of the journal believed that the results were supported by valid evidence, then it was appropriate to publish the study—but odd not to offer editorial comment. On the other hand, if the editors did not find the evidence convincing, then it is odd that they would choose to publish the study.

8. Faith-healing studies encourage the use of intercessory prayer, a technique that is widely used for questionable purposes. The intercessory prayer as described in the Cha study is similar to the intercessory prayer described in the book *Operation World: The Day-by-Day Guide to Praying for the World*.[15] This book, with more than 1 million copies in print, describes how intercessory prayer can and should be used to "take the kingdoms of this world for Jesus" and "challenge self-seeking sinners and bind or remove those who defy our God." Another popular book on prayer techniques, with hundreds of thousands of copies in print, explains that the fundamental purpose of intercessory prayer is to "hasten the day of total world evangelization" and thus complete the Great Commission of Jesus.[16] The same book also explains how thousands of Christian "prayer warriors" are using daily intercessory prayer in an effort to bring millions of unsaved souls in countries like China and Korea to Jesus. Can prayer for healing be divorced from prayer for salvation? For what reasons do the participants in the various Christian prayer groups in the Cha study generally use intercessory prayer when they are not taking part in an infertility study? One wonders if the Christian prayer group participants, with all the best intentions, were also praying for the salvation (conversion) of the Korean study subjects. Were they specifically instructed not to do so? In light of their strong Christian faith, could they ethically honor such a request even if it were made? Many of the prayer group participants may have sincerely believed that God would redeem or heal the Korean patients only if the patients accepted Jesus Christ as their savior.

Another book on intercessory prayer preaches that prayer is "the armor for every believer . . . the weapon of our warfare . . . for pulling down the strongholds of the enemy."[17] This same book also states that Christian intercessory prayers for both healing and fertility are intimately intertwined with prayers for salvation. To many evangelical Christians it might seem senseless or even sacrilegious to pray for the restoration of fertility to infidels or people with views heretical to the Christian faith, without first praying for their salvation. In his best-selling book *Healing*, Catholic priest Francis MacNutt states that "healing is simply the practical application of the basic Christian message of salvation." He also explains that "the first condition, if we seek healing, is to cast out sin" and that "what I have come to see, though, is how intimately the forgiveness of sins is connected with bodily and emotional healing. They are not separate. In fact, physical sickness is a direct sign that we are not right with God."[18] Now that it has been published in a peer-reviewed medical journal, the Cha study is certain to be used by Operation World proponents and other Christian evangelists as a compelling testimonial to the efficacy and power of intercessory prayer.

9. Positive faith-healing studies could affect public policy. President George W. Bush's stand in favor of faith-based initiatives has caused some Americans to believe that the Constitutional separation of church and state is in jeopardy. The conclusions of the Cha study may generate interest among policymakers who favor broadening the role of faith and prayer in the United States. . . .

10. Faith-healing studies could have emotional and psychological consequences for infertility patients. Emotional stress combined with fear of treatment failure can lead to serious depression in women with impaired fertility.[19] The psychological stress may become even more severe when all initial efforts to correct infertility fail and IVF is required. If this method of last resort fails, patients may lose hope and become despondent. Because of this, some experts recommend psychological counseling for patients who fail IVF.[20] If a patient were led to believe that God, rather than medical conditions, controlled the outcome of infertility treatments, then IVF failure could have severe emotional and psychological consequences. The already depressed woman would be burdened with the belief that her unworthiness and/or lack of faith had destroyed her chances for pregnancy and childbirth. The introduction to *An Intercessor's Handbook of Scriptural Prayers* states, "Prayer does not cause faith to work, but faith causes prayer to work. Therefore, any prayer problem is a problem of doubt—doubting the integrity of the Word and the ability of God to stand behind His promises or the statements of fact in the Word." In his book on healing by prayer, Father MacNutt agrees that "lack of faith" is the number one reason why God does not heal people and that sin is a close runner-up.

11. Faith-healing studies are self-perpetuating. If a faith-healing study successfully makes its way into a medical journal, its results will be used to promote faith healing even if its methods are hopelessly flawed and the results are not reproducible. For example, I recently wrote a letter to the editor of *Southern California Physician* critical of their article "Prescription for Prayer" and the claim by Larry Dossey, MD, that some 1,600 studies have revealed "something positive" about intercessory prayer. I commented that if there were, in fact, something positive, it certainly would not take 1,600 studies to find it. Dr. Dossey's published response to my letter included the following argument: "Controlled clinical trials and the peer-review process continue to serve us well. The most recent example of this process in action in the area of intercessory prayer is from Columbia Medical School—a positive, controlled clinical trial published in the respected, peer-reviewed *Journal of Reproductive Medicine*."[21] The flawed and possibly fraudulent Cha study has also been cited in other journals including the peer-reviewed *Journal of the American College of Surgeons* as strong evidence for the healing power of prayer.[22]

12. Birds of a feather flock together. Many faith-healing researchers also conduct research on other supernatural or paranormal phenomena. Of the 3 authors of the Cha study, Kwang Cha, MD, is a doctor from Korea who also practices in the United States and Rogerio Lobo, MD, is chairman of Obstetrics and Gynecology at Columbia University. Dr. Lobo now claims not to have been involved with the study until after its completion, stating that he provided only editorial assistance. The fact that 1 of the 3 authors now claims to have had nothing to do with the study is disturbing. Dr. Cha and Dr. Lobo both failed to respond to numerous telephone calls and letters requesting further information about their study. The remaining author, Daniel Wirth, MS, JD, has a long history of publishing studies on supernatural or paranormal phenomena, and his MS degree is in the dubious field of parapsychology. While doing research for this manuscript I discovered that the Federal Bureau of Investigation had indicted Mr. Wirth, claiming that he had conspired with ex-convict Joseph Horvath (AKA Joseph Hessler, AKA John Truelove, AKA John Doe) to defraud millions of dollars from the cable company Adelphia. Mr. Wirth initially denied knowing Horvath.

An Associated Press article on the indictment includes the following statement: "The FBI, in the embezzlement indictment against Wirth and John Doe, said Wirth lied when he told agents in July that he didn't know Truelove by any other last name."[23] After reading this article I reviewed my file of publications authored by Mr. Wirth. These publications deal with "paranormal" or apparently supernatural phenomena, including various topics such as "distant healing" and "prayer healing." I found an article from a little-known journal that claims to be devoted to "topics outside the established disciplines of mainstream science." The journal is the *International Journal of Scientific Exploration*. The article is "The Effect of Alternative Healing Therapy on the Regeneration Rate of Salamander Forelimbs." The coauthors are Daniel Wirth and Joseph Horvath.

In May 2004, both Wirth and Horvath pleaded guilty in federal court to criminal fraud and to using numerous phony identities to commit felonies. Only July 13, 2004, Horvath hanged himself in his prison cell. On November 23, 2004, Daniel Wirth was sentenced to five years in federal prison to be followed by three years of parole. He is currently incarcerated in a federal penitentiary in California.

Conclusion

As demonstrated in this article, there are dangers in the publication of studies that advocate faith healing. Although the Cha study demonstrates many of these dangers, the purpose of this critique is not to imply that only scoundrels conduct such studies. Undoubtedly, many religious individuals conduct faith-based studies with the best of intentions. Nevertheless, the fact remains that extraordinary claims demand extraordinary evidence. Unless replicated under strictly controlled conditions, studies claiming to have demonstrated miracle cures belong in religious magazines, not medical journals. Editors of medical journals and doctors who review manuscripts for journals should remember this obvious fact. Physicians take an oath to respect the hard-won scientific gains of those physicians in whose footsteps we walk. This is the first premise of the modern version of the Hippocratic Oath.

Notes
1. K.Y. Cha, D.B. Wirth, and R.A. Lobo, "Does Prayer Influence the Success of In Vitro Fertilization–Embryo Transfer?" *J Reprod Med*, no. 46, 2001, pp. 781–787.

2. B.L. Flamm, "Faith Healing by Prayer: Review of Cha, K.Y., Wirth, D.P., Lobo, R.A. 'Does Prayer Influence the Success of In Vitro Fertilization–Embryo Transfer?'" *Sci Rev Alt Med*, vol. 6, no. 1, 2002, pp. 47–50.

3. B.L. Flamm, "Faith Healing Confronts Modern Medicine," *Sci Rev Alt Med*, vol. 8, no. 1, 2004, pp. 9–14.

4. M. Schorr, "Prayer May Boost In-Vitro Success, Study Suggests," Reuters, October 8, 2001.

5. E. Nagourney, "Study Links Prayer and Pregnancy," *New York Times*, October 2, 2001.

6. T. Johnson, "Praying for Pregnancy: Study Says Prayer Helps Women Get Pregnant," *Good Morning America*, October 4, 2001.

7. N.L. Stotlland, "When Religion Collides with Medicine," *Am J Psychiatry*, no. 156, 1999, pp. 304–307.

8. S.M. Asser and R. Swan, "Child Fatalities from Religion-Motivated Medical Neglect," *Pediatrics*, no. 101, 1998, pp. 625–29.

9. J. Collins, "Cost-effectiveness of In-Vitro Fertilization," *Semin Reprod Med*, vol. 19, no. 3, 2001, pp. 279–90.

10. D.P. Wirth and J.R. Cram, "The Psychophysiology of Nontraditional Prayer," *Int J Psychosom*, vol. 41, nos. 1–4, 1994, pp. 68–75.

11. D.P. Wirth and J.R. Cram, "Multi-Site Electromyographic Analysis of Non-Contact Therapeutic Touch," *Int J Psychosom*, vol. 40, nos. 1–4, 1993, pp. 47–55.

12. D.P. Wirth and M.J. Marrett, "Complementary Healing Therapies," *Int J Psychosom*, vol. 41, nos. 1–4, 1994, pp. 61–67.

13. D.P. Wirth, "The Significance of Belief and Expectancy Within the Spiritual Healing Encounter," *Soc Sci Med*, vol. 41, no. 2, 1995, pp. 249–60.

14. D.P. Wirth, J.T. Richardson, and W.S. Eidelman, "Wound Healing and Complementary Therapies: A Review," *J Altern Complement Med*, vol. 2, no. 4, 1996, pp. 493–502.

15. P. Johnstone, *Operation World: The Day-by-Day Guide to Praying for the World*. Grand Rapids, MI: Zondervan, 1993.

16. D. Eastman, *The Hour That Changes the World: A Practical Plan for Personal Prayer*. Mission Hills, CA: Baker, 1988.

17. C. Copeland, *Prayers That Avail Much: An Intercessor's Handbook of Scriptural Prayers*. Tulsa, OK: Harrison House, 1987.

18. F. MacNutt, *Healing: The Most Comprehensive Book Ever Written on Healing Through Prayer*. New York: Bantam, 1980.

19. J. Hunt, and J.H. Monach, "Beyond the Bereavement Model: The Significance of Depression for Infertility Counseling," *Hum Reprod*, vol. 12, no. 11, 1997, pp. 188–94.

20. B.S. Kee, B.J. Jung, and S.H. Lee, "A Study on Psychological Strain in IVF Patients," *J Assist Reprod Genet*, vol. 17, no. 8, 2000, pp. 445–51.

21. L. Dossey, "Prescription for Prayer," *Southern California Physician*, December 2001, p. 46.

22. J.L. Tarpley and M.J. Tarpley, "Spirituality in Surgical Practice," *J Am Coll Surg*, vol. 194, no. 5, 2002, pp. 642–647.

23. M. Dale, "Anderson Added to Changes Pending Against Ex-Adelphia Manager," Associated Press, February 5, 2003.

Faith Healing Has No Place in Modern Medicine

Timothy N. Gorski

In the following viewpoint Timothy N. Gorski rejects the idea that faith healing has a place in modern medicine. Faith healing would serve to alienate those who do not believe in miraculous healings, he argues. Gorski points out that health care does not discourage patients from seeking outside spiritual guidance.

Gorski is a practicing gynecologist in Dallas, Texas. He has served as the president of the Dallas/Fort Worth Council Against Health Fraud as well as on the board of the National Council Against Health Fraud. He is also an associate editor of the Scientific Review of Alternative Medicine.

Religious and spiritual concerns have traditionally been in the background in American healthcare, which has relied largely on medical science for guidance. But the medical subordination of such concerns has never given health professionals or healthcare administrators in the United States license to belittle or ignore religious beliefs and practices, which are integral to many persons' sense of well-being. More to the point, it has never meant that patients could not turn to religious practices, or to clerics, for comfort as adjuncts to medical care. Importantly, it has facilitated health professionals' maintaining detachment from patients' religious and private spiritual matters.

This is as it should be, in light of how subjective religious opinions are, how deep-rooted they can be, and their extraordinary diversity in the U.S. If religious and spiritual concerns

Timothy N. Gorski, "Should Religion and Spiritual Concerns Be More Influential in American Healthcare? No.", *Priorities*, vol. 12, March 1, 2000. Copyright © 2000 American Council on Science and Health. All rights reserved. Reproduced with permission of American Council on Science and Health (ACSH). For more information on ACSH visit www.acsh.org.

became more influential in medicine, effective, ethical, compassionate healthcare would suffer. Incorporating religion with medicine would be inconsistent with major ideals of the medical profession:

Objectivity

A substantial increase in religion's influence on healthcare would result in a decrease in objectivity and impartiality among medical professionals.

Religious Nonpartisanship

How can healthcare practitioners actively support their patients' diverse religious beliefs and practices without hypocrisy; without offending patients who do not subscribe to certain of such beliefs; and without offending atheists, agnostics, and religious nonaffiliates, who together constitute a significant proportion of the American population?

In no interfaith, nondenominational, or multicultural healthcare setting can a medical professional exhibit an appeal to Allah without diminishing non-Islamic mainstream religious principles. It is likewise impossible to pray conspicuously to the Virgin Mary or to Roman Catholic saints without encroaching on Protestant beliefs. Many Christians regard even spiritual practices that are neo-Christian, nondenominational, and/or eclectic—particularly those associated with the New Age movement—as harmful, if not devil-inspired. Allegiance to ecclesiastic principles has led to calls for boycotts against Disney and even the U.S. military. Unless American healthcare becomes balkanized on the basis of religious creeds, a substantial increase in religion's influence on medicine would lead to hypocrisy, factionalism, and partisanship within hospitals and clinics.

Those who doubt that increasing religion's influence in healthcare would be divisive can easily rid themselves of such doubt, by becoming informed of recent events in which the intersection of religion and medicine has been crucial—for example, the firing of a physician based on his having submitted a letter to a local newspaper editor that conveyed views his employer described as contrary to fundamental Roman Catholic teachings; the scuttling of hospital-merger plans because of religious orders' steadfast demands concerning what medical services are ecclesiastically acceptable; and clashes over "assisted reproduction," abortion, euthanasia, and other issues on which there is no universal religious consensus. Indeed, the prospect of the spiritualizing of healthcare is appealing only to the extent that one associates such expressions as "religion" and "spirituality" with one's subjective religious and spiritual beliefs.

Nonmaleficence and Beneficence

Health professionals have a dual responsibility to their patients: to "do no harm" (nonmaleficence) and to act according to the best interests of each patient (beneficence). Both whether religion can improve health and what risks religion may entail are far from determined. Incorporating religion with medicine raises serious questions of medical ethics.

For example, although it appears that churchgoers tend to be healthier and more long-lived than nonchurchgoers, even incontrovertible proof that churchgoers are healthier and more long-lived would hardly constitute a sound basis for the contention that churchgoing per se is responsible for these advantages. The association apparently does not depend on what church is attended. Thus, social connectedness may be at least partly responsible for it. And healthier segments of the American population—e.g., the married, the occupationally satisfied, and the prominent—may tend to be more socially connected. Moreover, perhaps individuals who are healthy and socially well connected are more disposed to churchgoing than are unhealthy, poorly socially connected persons. Therefore, churchgoers may attend religious services partly because they are relatively healthy and partly because they are well connected socially. On the other hand, many of the reasons religiously nonobservant persons have for this nonobservance—for example, familial religious discord—may be such that churchgoing would be unhealthful for them.

Until such questions of causality and contraindications are answered scientifically—if they can be—it is dangerous and ethically unacceptable for healthcare practitioners to counsel patients on spiritual matters. And it might well be so even if such questions were properly and exhaustively answered. For example, would scientific research establishing that believing in Allah is more therapeutic than is believing in Buddha, Yahweh, Jesus, or the Hindu pantheon constitute adequate grounds for medical professionals' promoting Islam to patients over religions associated with the other alleged divine spirits? Furthermore, would scientifically establishing that undergoing a crisis of religious doubt carries serious health risks make it appropriate to deal with such doubt as pathologic and medically remediable? And if it were appropriate, could medical professionals credibly claim an objective understanding of what is best for patients concerning religion?

Patients' Autonomy

Increasing religion's influence in healthcare would diminish the autonomy of patients. It is incumbent on physicians to know the health advantages and health risks to individual patients of each of numerous validated interventions, and to be prepared to convey such information intelligibly to patients so that the patients can make informed decisions. In matters of religion, however, a hands-off policy should continue to prevail among health professionals, except when the potential health consequences of particular religious behaviors are clearcut and adverse to the patient—for example, a patient's refusal of a blood transfusion without which he or she would die, or parents' rejection of critical medical care for their underage children.

When the prospective health consequences of particular religious behaviors are not clear-cut, and when they are not adverse to the patient, the religious views and spiritual suggestions of medical professionals are extraneous. Indeed, expressions of such opinions may be unwelcome and, even if they are welcome initially, may introduce coercion into the physician-patient relationship. It is out of a respect for patients' autonomy that the rule of nonjudgmental noninterference has been established for such eventualities as certain nonreligious cultural practices, unusual sex acts, childbearing in various hazardous circumstances (e.g., of the patient's making), and even, to some degree, "recreational drug use." It is ironic that in such cases medical professionals respect individuals' lifestyle choices, for good or ill, as an ethical obligation, while it is seriously and widely proposed that such professionals should urge their patients to pray, attend religious services, and embrace various supernatural beliefs. Aren't religion and spirituality at least as intimate as sexuality, the instinct to reproduce, and nonreligious cultural aspects of personality?

Humanism

Biomedicine is rooted both in science and in humanism—a philosophy that promotes, for example, not only consideration for the sick and understanding and tolerance of religious beliefs and practices in general, but also acceptance of the rights of conscience of nonreligious persons. Consistency with this long-standing aspect of modern medicine requires that health-care professionals distance themselves from any purely religious issues that may arise in the context of their duties; it certainly demands that such professionals forbear from promoting and/or challenging religious beliefs, whatever their patients may want in the way of medico-spiritual counseling.

The grave of four-day-old Michael Boehmer in Lake City, Florida, December 8, 2004. Michael died of lack of blood from a nosebleed. The bleeding could have been stopped by a vitamin K shot, but his parents, who followed "End Time" religion, do not use doctors, and instead rely on prayer and faith healing. AP Images

It is very likely that an expansion of the role of religion in healthcare would not humanize medical care but rather would erode, perhaps even devastate, the physician-patient relationship, which has always been the cornerstone of compassionate medical care. A 1999 edition of the Texan paper *The Arlington Morning News* quoted a hometown girl who had recently graduated high school: "I want to be a pediatric surgeon because I really love little kids, and if you work on little kids and they die, then you at least know they will go to heaven since they haven't had time to do anything wrong in their life." The sentiments behind this statement were undoubtedly innocent—but would such an expression comfort parents with a desperately ill child being prepped for surgery? And suppose the parents' afterlife-related beliefs differ markedly from those that the surgeon's statements suggest?

There are many other risks—subtler than those of diminishing patients' autonomy and privacy—inherent in the encroachment of religion on medicine. For example, how would the role of clergy change? How would relationships change in interfaith households and among friends of different theologies? The effects would be unpredictable and, especially in cases of grave illness, could be perilous. If healthcare professionals—who themselves have disparate religious, antireligious, and secular philosophies—were constrained to incorporate religion and spirituality in their practices, certainly they would do so differently, and with scarce scientific grounds for such disparities. Healthcare practitioners simply have no right to influence directly and deliberately the spiritual aspects of patients' lives.

Keeping Medicine and Faith Separate

In healthcare there are numerous occasions for misunderstandings that can undermine the often fragile physician-patient relationship. A physician's mispronouncing a patient's name, addressing a patient by the wrong name, or momentarily forgetting what a patient has just said, for example, can alone put a dent in their relationship. Physicians' spiritually pontificating, sermonizing, or even just neutrally broaching specific religious concepts can only make matters worse. For instance, how might a patient—particularly a religious non-Christian patient—react if a physician asked him or her: "Have you accepted Jesus Christ as your personal savior?"

Traditionally, recourse to religion or to spiritual practices has figured in biomedical settings in developed countries only in cases of grave, intractable, or incurable illness. But many formerly grave, intractable, or incurable diseases are very treatable; and it is because those ostensible explanations and remedies that were religious did not satisfy medical professionals that there has been progress against formerly untreatable diseases.

By distancing itself somewhat from religion and spiritual concerns, American healthcare avoids stepping on spiritual and other toes. Incorporating religion with medicine would ultimately please no one. Unions of religious and governmental bodies have long tended to be calamitous. There is no good reason to believe that expanding American healthcare's religious or spiritual features would have different results.

Pentecostal Faith Healers Are Fakes

Keith Gibson

In the following article Keith Gibson exposes well-known Pentacostal faith healer Benny Hinn as a fake. He argues that Hinn is nothing more than a showman with cheap tricks. Gibson reveals the reasons people feel that they are healed and points out the problems associated with falsely believing that a faith healing has taken place.

Gibson is ordained in the Southern Baptist Church and has been a minister for twenty years. He speaks at a variety of conferences and is currently pursuing a doctorate in theology.

Among the celebrities in the Word Faith Movement, none is more well known than Benny Hinn. From his lavish life-style to his on-stage performances, Benny Hinn has become the modern stereotype of the faith healers, even providing at least partial inspiration for Steve Martin's character in the movie *Leap of Faith*. Hinn claims that thousands have been healed in his crusades. There have even been claims of the dead being raised. But when pressed for documentation, the ministry has been woefully unable to provide much, if any, evidence for these assertions. Despite years of exposés by both Christian and secular sources alike, his ministry continues to have thousands of ardent followers. It is estimated by various sources that his organization takes in over one hundred million dollars per year, though this amount is disputed and is impossible to verify as the ministry refuses to publicly disclose its finances. . . .

Keith Gibson, "Faith Healers or Fake Healers?" *Apologetics Resource Center*, vol. 3, no. 6, November–December 2003. © 2003 Apologetics Resource Center. All rights reserved. This article was originally published in *Areopagus Journal*. Used by permission.

A Comparison to Christ

One way to evaluate whether or not ministers like Hinn possess healing power would be to compare their miracles to those of Christ. When this is done, striking differences begin to appear. First, Christ healed specific individuals. Never once do we read a passage where Jesus says anything like,

> A muscle condition has been healed. I give you the praise. Just now lift your hands and call upon His precious name, dear Jesus, dear Jesus, dear Jesus. Sinuses have just been healed, I give you praise. A neck injury has been healed, I give you the praise. In the audience God is touching people right now right here, the Lord is touching many of you in this audience right here in this studio, I give you praise, Jesus. In your homes, many of you are being healed. Someone's shoulders have just been released from pain, someone with a shoulder problem has just been healed, I give you praise, Jesus.[1]

Yet this is standard fare among healers like Hinn who regularly stands at the front of the auditorium and recites illnesses supposedly being healed as though he is taking roll. Those who think they are among the recipients of healing are then invited to come to the front to testify.

It should be noted too that all of this is carefully orchestrated by Hinn's associates. Many who are not considered a good healing risk are restricted from access to Hinn. Dr. Stephen Winzenburg, a professor at Grand View College in Des Moines, Iowa has conducted research into evangelists' ministries. Concerning Hinn, Dr. Winzenburg states, "He's very much like a circus ringmaster when he's there in the arena. People may be coming for healing, but it's very much controlled hysteria."[2] . . .

An HBO [television network] special documented Hinn's crusade in Portland, Oregon. On stage Hinn performed 76 alleged miracles. The documentary's producers asked the ministry for the names of the healed. Thirteen weeks later, only five names were received. Upon investigation, none had received an actual healing. One of those was 10-year-old Ashmil Prakash who had been stricken with two brain tumors. Despite the "healing" pronounced by Hinn and the pledge made by his impoverished parents to give thousands of dollars to Hinn's ministry, the child died seven weeks after the crusade.[3]

Lastly, the healings of Jesus were not psychosomatic. Jesus raised the dead and gave sight to those born blind and lame. Despite the claims, no good documentation exists that any of today's healers have done similar miracles. The sad fact is they can't even heal their own family members. Hinn's mother was diabetic and his father died of cancer.[4] The stories of other faith healers are similar.

What Is Going On?

So what is one to make of all of the testimonies of miraculous occurrences? What of all those who every day are paraded on a host of shows on TBN [Trinity Broadcasting Network] and other networks, including Hinn's own, *This Is Your Day?* Several items must be considered by the discerning Christian.

Some of the healings are psychosomatic. People whose primary problems are psychosocial in nature respond positively to placebo effects such as faith healers. In fact, the entire atmosphere of the crusades is orchestrated to build to a climax at the appearance of Hinn and the healing touch. Jesus never had to set the mood in order to be able to work. These emotionally charged events can have great impact on those whose conditions are more psychological than physical.

Many are not healed at all. Having a person stand on stage and claim to be healed of cancer or other ailment doesn't prove the healing has actually taken place. Such healings should be verified by a qualified physician using proper medical studies. These claims to healing can be the result of:

> Temporary euphoria—many people are caught up in the
> moment. The adrenaline rush and anticipation, even the ex-

citement of being in the presence of one considered so anointed, may be enough to provide momentary relief. This is especially true of conditions whose primary symptom is pain.

Positive Confession—what happens at these crusades cannot be separated from a theology that teaches its adherents they possess what they confess. In the belief system of many of these people, to confess that they are not yet healed would be to guarantee that they wouldn't receive it. Many of them are simply confessing what they believe they will receive at some point.

Hero Worship—There is tremendous desire on the part of many of these participants not to embarrass the healer. They believe so much in the person that they will react as they are instructed, even when they know it is not true. Consider the story of a woman supposedly healed of blindness by Oral Roberts. When instructed by Roberts onstage, "Tell us what's happening inside you." She replied, "There—There was a light." However when interviewed the next day she admitted that nothing had happened. She stated simply, "I didn't want to disappoint him."[5]

Some are outright fakes. James Randi, a magician, in his book, *Faith Healers*, documents many of the tactics used to deceive the gullible. Some are as simple as placing staffers in the audience who pretend to be healed. W.V. Grant would pull the heel of one shoe out slightly to make it appear that he was lengthening a leg. Peter Popoff received his "Words of knowledge" through a transistor in his ear through which his wife, via radio transmission, instructed him as she read from cards collected by staffers. Several faith healers have rented wheelchairs to use as props. Some have even encouraged people who walked into the crusade to sit in one of these chairs so they could be taken up to the front to get a better view. These same people were then pulled out of their wheelchairs to the amazement of the crowds.[6] The list of tricks is almost endless.

Some are natural occurrences. The fact is that many illnesses get better naturally. This is true regardless of the treatment provided and sometimes without any treatment at all. These, then, are not miraculous healings, but rather the result of the wonderful way humans have been created by an all-wise God. For instance, ninety percent of all patients with low back pain will recover in approximately six weeks regardless of whether the pain was caused by a simple strain or a herniated, degenerative or bulging disc.[7] Even cancer has been known to have spontaneous remissions. These occur among believers and unbelievers alike, people who were prayed for as well as those who weren't, and are presently without medical explanation.[8] . . .

Concerns

So what's the problem anyway? False hope is better than no hope right? Maybe Benny can't heal but who's he hurting? Perhaps we should just leave him alone.

But people are hurt. False hope is actually devastating. Listen to the words of Brian Darby, who works with the handicapped in Northern California: "You can't minimize the impact of not being healed on the person, the family, the extended family. . . . They have a sense of euphoria at the crusade and then crash down."[9] The effect of not being healed can be terribly disillusioning. However, healers such as Hinn can always deflect criticism by blaming the sick for not having enough faith.

And what about those who might stop taking essential medication thinking they have been healed without medical verification? On the September 30, 2003, episode of Hinn's, *This Is Your Day*, a young woman is brought to the platform with what appears to be a blood sugar test kit. It is referred to by Steve Brock as her diabetes "pack". After stating that God has healed her, she proceeds to throw the pack down on the floor of the platform. Left untreated, diabetes can cause a host of debilitating medical complications and ultimately death. One sincerely hopes this young lady visits her physician to verify her healing. Healings of diseases such as diabetes and cancer cannot be validated within the confines of the crusades. There is serious concern for the welfare of many claiming healing.

Notes

1. Quoted in Sandy Simpson, "Benny Hinn's Response to *Dateline NBC*," November 1, 2003. www.deceptioninthechurch.com/hinndatelineresponse.html.
2. Quoted in Kamon Simpson, "Benny Hinn: Faith Healer or Fraud?" *Kansas City Star*, August 8, 2003.
3. M. Kurt Goedelman, "Hinn, Bonnke Focus of HBO Special," 2001. www.pfo.org/hinnhbo.
4. Goedelman, "Hinn, Bonnke Focus of HBO Special."
5. C. Fisher and M. Kurt Goedelman, *The Confusing World of Benny Hinn*. St. Louis: Personal Freedom Outreach, p. 111.
6. James Randi, *The Faith Healers*. Buffalo, NY: Prometheus 1987.
7. Spine-health.com, "Treatment of Low Back Pain," 2000.
8. Norman Geisler, *Signs and Wonders*. Toronto: Tyndale, 1988, p. 56.
9. William Lobdell, "The Price of Healing," *Los Angeles Times Magazine*, July 2003.

Epilogue: Analyzing the Evidence

Faith healing has long been a subject of debate. Each of the articles presented in this book make a case either for or against the reality of faith healings. Additionally, some of the articles also either advocate or discourage the advancement of faith in modern medical practice. Faith healing often involves religion, and so it is a subject that raises strong feelings in both advocates and detractors. Someone who believes that he or she has experienced a miraculous healing has a perspective that differs substantially from someone who insists that all healing is the result of a natural process.

With so much information about one topic, it can be difficult to determine which arguments are the most valid. Not only is there a great deal of information, but for every credible expert on one side of the question, there is another equally credible expert on the other side of the argument. Ultimately, your position on the question of the existence of viable faith healing depends upon your ability to critically read and analyze the information presented.

The purpose of this epilogue is to help you understand the methods by which you can evaluate the evidence you have been presented and come to your own conclusion. Rather than tell you whether faith healings are real and useful, this epilogue will guide you through the process of examining the evidence through critical reading and then coming to a decision that best fits your understanding and analysis of the information provided.

Who Is the Author?

One of the first considerations in critical reading is the source of your information. The author of the article provides valuable clues as to how credible the article is. An argument's quality cannot be determined solely on the background and credentials of the person who wrote it, but it is possible to better understand the likelihood that the article has been well researched.

Questions you should ask yourself about the author include the following: Does the author have a reputation as an accurate researcher? Does the author's background include qualifications to write authoritatively on the subject? Has the author witnessed a faith healing or received one? Has the author witnessed any ill effects as a result of reliance on faith healing? Are there noticeable biases in the author's writing? All of these questions can help you decide how much weight to give to a particular author's argument.

Critical Reading and Analysis

Critical reading and analysis is based on a five-step approach known as hypothetical reasoning. Scientists and philosophers often use this approach to determine the merits of a case, argument, or theory. Even if you are unsure as to how reliable an author is, it is possible to decide on the reasonableness of an argument by carefully considering the evidence given in support of the argument. You should understand, however, that hypothetical reasoning does not constitute the truth of a claim. Rather, it provides a way for you to critically examine the information presented and come to your own conclusion as to whether the argument makes sense.

Here are the five steps of hypothetical reasoning:

1. State the author's main argument (the hypothesis).
2. Gather the evidence the author uses to support the argument.
3. Examine the gathered evidence.
4. Consider alternative arguments.
5. Draw your own conclusion about the validity of the author's argument.

Just because you have followed the process of hypothetical reasoning does not mean that you will have certainty. Some doubts one way or the other may remain, and it is up to you whether you would like to suspend judgment until you have a chance to find more information on the subject. When evaluating two articles on the same subject, but that express different viewpoints, you can use this process to compare the two and decide for yourself which you think to be more reasonable.

The following sections will help you become comfortable with the process of hypothetical reasoning. We will use the process of critical reading and analysis to evaluate two of the articles in this book. You can then apply the principles to other articles in this book and to other arguments you come in contact with.

1. State the Author's Hypothesis

A hypothesis is a statement that can be tested in order to decide how likely its claim of truth is. In order to critically analyze an article, it is important for you to test the hypothesis made by the author. Each of the articles in this book deals with faith healing. In order to begin critically examining each article's reasonableness, you should begin by listing each author with his or her main argument. The title of each article provides clues as to what the hypothesis is. A table, like the one below, can help you easily organize information. Four authors in the table do not have hypotheses listed next to their names. Try to determine each author's hypothesis and complete the table.

Author	Hypothesis
Reginald O. Crosby	Healing by miraculous means (faith) is a reality
Jeff Levin	The use of prayer can heal illness
Harold Koenig	
Jeffrey Barg interview with Eve Wood	
Allan Anderson	Pentecostal faith healing exists

Author	Hypothesis
John A. Henderson	Miracles (including faith healing) are not real
Richard Sloan, Emilia Bagiella, Tia Powell	
Bruce L. Flamm	Faith healing can harm patients physically, mentally, and emotionally
Timothy N. Gorski	Faith is incompatible with modern medical practice and its values and ethics
Keith Gibson	

As you evaluate the hypotheses, you should keep in mind that there are three specific criteria for a good hypothesis. A hypothesis should be clear, specific, and provable (or disprovable).

Clear: A clear hypothesis is one that is fairly obvious and stated concisely.

Specific: When a hypothesis is specific, it states a particular claim rather than a broad generalization. Rather than say "Faith healing can harm patients physically, mentally, and emotionally," the specific evils that the article points to are listed.

Provable (or disprovable): In theory, you should be able to prove or disprove the hypothesis. It should be an alleged fact, stated with certainty. You can then evaluate the evidence and decide whether it proves or disproves the hypothesis.

Now we will go through the hypothetical reasoning process with one "for" article and one "against" article to practice critical reading and analysis skills.

Harold Koenig: "Faith Has a Positive Effect on Patients"

1. State the author's hypothesis. Religious faith can offer a degree of protection from physical and emotional illness.

2. Gather the evidence the author uses to support the argument. Once you have determined the hypothesis, your next

101

step is to gather the evidence that supports the author's main argument. Anything that the author uses to prove that the claim is true should be used. Here is some of the evidence from the third article in Chapter 1:

1. Koenig is a medical doctor.

2. Personal observation of three patients who used faith to improve their medical circumstances shows that faith had a positive effect on health.

3. Conducted a study and found those with personal faith felt less death anxiety to a degree that was statistically significant.

4. Personally led or participated in many additional studies linking faith and health that passed the peer-review process and were published in scientific and medical journals. The findings from these studies include:

    a. Lower blood pressure results from personal prayer, church attendance, and Bible study.

    b. Religious people have healthier lifestyles.

    c. People with strong faith who go through physical illness have better health outcomes than those without strong faith.

    d. Religious people have stronger immune systems.

3. Examine the gathered evidence. Now that we have the evidence, it is time to determine how strong the evidence supporting the author's main argument is.

Statements of fact (list items 1, 3, and 4). A fact is a claim that can be verified. Many claims are easy to verify with reference materials. Some statements, however, are not so easy to verify. In such cases, it is possible to apply the process of hypothetical reasoning to that particular fact and determine its reasonableness. The statements of fact in this example are fairly easy to verify. Koenig is a medical doctor, and the studies were, in fact, conducted, peer-reviewed, and published.

Generalizations (items 4a through 4d). A generalization makes use of examples to make its claim. If an author uses four examples of people who enjoy eating chocolate, a generalization might be made that all people enjoy eating chocolate. Despite the obvious problems with generalizations, they are nevertheless important parts of the reasoning process. There are two main types of generalization: explicit and implicit. An explicit generalization is one in which the author directly argues the truth of a generalized claim. An implicit generalization is one in which the author provides information that logically leads the reader to generalize.

Combined, the items 4a through 4d lead the reader to implicitly generalize that he or she will enjoy better health and less sickness by adhering to religious faith. Each of these items individually and explicitly generalizes that following certain practices leads to specific health outcomes.

Eyewitness testimony (item 2). Eyewitness testimony plays a large part in the way we perceive our world. Journalists provide us with eyewitness accounts of current events. Recorded eyewitness testimony from ancient times through the present form the basis for our historical knowledge. We tend to place great weight on information that comes from people who "saw it themselves."

Eyewitness testimony has a substantial drawback, however. It is easy to fabricate. A lying eyewitness immediately leads the critical reader astray. And that is not the only problem. Many eyewitnesses are inaccurate through more honest means: mistakes, being fooled, remembering incorrectly, and hallucinations. There is no malice in any of these, but the witness is wrong. Here are two factors that you can consider when deciding whether or not to trust the eye witness:

1. Witness credibility. First, try to discover if the witness has a record of dishonest or unreliable behavior. If the witness is generally honest and accurate, then he or she is likely to be credible in the circumstance at

hand. Also, you should study any credentials the witness has that are relevant to the question. Other issues that affect witness credibility include unusual stress (emotional, physical, or mental), intoxication at the time of the event, what the witness has to gain or lose, and possible bias.

2. Testimony credibility. If you decide that the witness is likely credible, it is time to turn to the testimony. Can the information be substantiated by another source? This source can be another eyewitness testimony or some documented evidence. You should also check for contradictions between sources of evidence, and also for contradictions within the account of the event itself. Too many significant contradictions are an indication that the testimony could be suspect. Koenig offers his personal eyewitness account of three different patients whose faith helped them get through some sort of medical condition. He believes that his observations support the idea that these patients experienced measures of faith healing on different levels. It is also worth noting (as you would find out with a little research) that Koenig started out skeptical of the role of faith in the patient healing process. Does this make him a more credible witness?

After reading the article and taking into account the fact that Koenig is a medical doctor, experienced in dealing with patients, and evaluating his eyewitness testimony, is it something you consider credible?

4. Consider alternative arguments. An important aspect of critical reading and analysis is to examine how an author addresses alternative explanations for the evidence presented. Many authors fail to address competing explanations. Some who do address alternative arguments do so in a way that is unfair or incomplete. Failure to address competing claims is often a sign that the author has not thoroughly supported his or her claim. A one-sided argument does not mean that the hypothesis is bad. However, an author should be confident that his or her explanation withstands scrutiny.

Pay attention to the tone with which an author describes alternative hypotheses. Is it patronizing or hostile? This can be an indication that the author wishes to use emotion rather than reason to sway you. Additionally, hostility and/or a patronizing tone can show that the author is not considering alternative explanations on a rational level.

Koenig does not go into great detail about viewpoints that oppose his. He cites a general Freudian attempt to describe religion as something used by neurotics. Additionally he references a study that he calls scornful of the idea that faith can help patients. While his language is not particularly harsh, Koenig does not address more moderate views that attitude, regardless of religious faith and practice, can have an effect on patients. He instead focuses on a view that is the extreme opposite and would naturally offend most readers.

5. Draw your own conclusion about the validity of the author's argument. Consider everything that you have learned about the article and its author. It is time to evaluate the strength of the argument made by the author. There are five main classifications that allow you to determine how you feel about the author's argument. It is not meant to evaluate the conclusion the author makes. Even if the ideas are bad, it is possible for the argument on their behalf to be good, and vice versa.

1. *Acceptance.* The author's argument is extremely convincing. You deem all of the points credible, and there are no major flaws in the argument.

2. *Limited acceptance.* There are noticeable flaws in the argument, but you find it somewhat convincing and credible.

3. *Neutral.* You remain unable to judge the author's argument. Perhaps you feel insufficient evidence has been

provided, or that it is inconclusive. Sometimes you can reach neutrality by virtue of not having knowledge of fields presented, or you feel unqualified to evaluate abstract concepts that may be listed.

4. *Limited disagreement.* Even though you find the argument weak, you feel that there is some merit, and that the argument warrants possible further discussion.

5. *Dismissal.* The important evidence presented in the piece is unconvincing. When examined critically, the argument falls apart and cannot be substantiated.

Where does Dr. Koenig's argument rank on this scale? What are the argument's strongest points? What are its weakest points? Is there any way you would improve the argument?

Bruce L. Flamm: "Reliance on Faith Healing Can Harm Patients"

1. State the author's main argument. Faith healing can harm patients physically, mentally, and emotionally.

2. Gather the evidence the author uses to support the argument.

1. The publication of articles supporting faith healing in medical journals can lead some patients, doctors, and insurance companies to conclude that prayer is more effective than medical treatment.

2. A recent study identified 158 children who died due to reliance on faith healing and religion-motivated medical neglect.

3. The Cha study, a study that offers evidence of the success of faith healing, was conducted without informed consent. The lack of informed consent skewed the results because patients were not informed of their participation in the study, even though the study pro-

moted Christian prayers in a Korean population that is majority Buddhist, Shamanist, or nonreligious.

4. Some of the people involved with the Cha study already believed in faith healing prior to the study's inception, which opens them up to a charge of bias.

5. The Cha study violated patients' privacy by circulating photos of them without their knowledge.

6. Intercessory prayer for healing is inextricably linked with the Christian faith and, by extension, prayer for the salvation of the patient. The study's support of this belief system is not scientifically-based and should not be promoted in a medical journal.

7. The publication of the Cha study in a medical journal could affect public policy by encouraging the expansion of faith-based initiatives based on scientific evidence.

8. The belief that the failure of intercessory prayer to achieve the desired physical healing is the result of the patient's lack of faith or a sin issue in his/her life can be emotionally crippling to a patient who is not healed.

9. Many faith-healing researchers use dubious evidence or studies conducted by like-minded individuals as support for their own findings.

10. One author of the Cha study now claims to have only offered editorial assistance at the end of the study. The second author has not responded to requests for further information, and third author is now serving time in prison for fraud.

3. Examine the gathered evidence. Bruce Flamm's article focuses on the ethical and political problems of publishing studies that support faith healings in medical journals, specifically referencing the Cha study. He argues that the promotion of faith healing in science-based journals incorrectly links a reli-

gious belief with scientific findings, which could result in patients, doctors, and policy-makers assuming that faith healing
and medical treatments are equal in terms of scientific basis
and effectiveness. Flamm uses statements of fact to discredit
the Cha study; expert testimonials in the form of his own
opinion as well as a separate study; and logic arguments.

Statements of fact (items 3–5, 9, 10). Flamm provides facts
about the Cha study that call into question its use as a scientific study. He points out that the study does not follow the
rigorous testing environment of other scientific studies; furthermore, the authorship of the study is questionable since
one of the principal authors was not involved in the actual
study, a second refuses to discuss his involvement, and a third
is a felon in jail for fraud. The Cha study is further discredited, according to Flamm, by the fact that the authors had a
pre-existing belief in faith healing, which diminishes their
ability to be unbiased in their approach to the study.

Expert testimonials (item 2). Under certain circumstances,
an opinion can be a convincing piece of evidence. Even though
opinions are considered among the weakest forms of evidence, if the opinion is given by an expert, in the form of a
testimonial, it can be quite convincing. In a legal court, an expert (someone who has a great deal of experience in a particular field) is often called to denounce or support a claim
based upon her or his experience, credentials, and reputation.
Here is how to weigh an expert testimonial:

1. Determine the expert's credentials. An expert testimonial is strongest when the expert is better qualified to
   give an opinion on a certain subject. If you or I tried
   to support a theory of astrophysics, chances are that
   we would not be taken very seriously. However,
   Stephen Hawking is considered an expert on astrophysics, and his opinion about a theory is considered
   convincing evidence.

2. Check for bias. It is important to understand someone's biases before completely accepting an expert testimonial. Even though the president of a company that disposes of nuclear waste may know more about storing it than the rest of us, many might be skeptical when he or she tells them that storing more contaminated waste within state boundaries would be perfectly safe.

3. Double-check an expert testimonial when possible. Sometimes the expert is quoted out of context to strengthen the argument. This can be done either intentionally or unintentionally, but it is important to make sure that the evidence is in its proper context.

Flamm makes use of expert testimonials in the forms of a study and his own expertise. Flamm, as a clinical medical professor, is qualified to look at medical studies and determine whether or not a study is conducted under rigorous scientific conditions or is open to charges of bias. The study, though not conducted by Barrett, might be considered compelling in its findings if you accept the expertise of those who conducted the study. Finally, Flamm's experience in the medical field has allowed him insight into the workings of medical insurance and patient care.

Do you think that Flamm's background, experience, and expertise make him a credible expert?

Logic arguments (items 1, 6–8). Flamm relies heavily on logic arguments in presenting his case against the publication of faith-healing studies in medical journals. Logic arguments are based on hypotheticals and logical conclusions that can be drawn from the hypotheticals. For instance, Flamm considers the ramifications of equating faith healing and and medical science, suggesting that patients, insurance companies, and the government would each experience a radical shift in policy and perspective were they to take the findings of the Cha study seriously. Based on the doubts about such studies raised by Flamm, these shifts seem ill-advised and even dangerous, yet the publication of the Cha study in a medical journal demands that these shifts be considered. Flamm also focuses on faith healing's close ties to Christianity and the logical problems this poses for people of other faiths and belief systems, as well as the psychological damage that is likely to occur when patients do not receive healing.

4. Consider alternative arguments. Flamm acknowledges that faith healing has a place within religious communities, but does not entertain the possibility that faith healing is a credible alternative to medical science.

5. Draw your own conclusion about the validity of the author's argument. Does Bruce Flamm's argument about the problems with faith healing seem reasonable? Has he made a good case for his position? How would you rank it on the five-point scale?

Now You Try It!

Choose an article from this book and analyze it using hypothetical reading to critically examine the piece. You can use this method for the rest of the articles in this book, or on articles from other sources.

Name of article _____ Author _____

1. State the author's main argument.
2. Find the main points of evidence and put them into a numbered list.
3. Examine the gathered evidence. Identify each type of evidence and evaluate it as we did in the previous two examples. Does it fall into the categories mentioned above? Or is it a different type of evidence?
4. Consider alternative arguments. Does the author offer any alternative arguments? Are they presented in a fair way?

What are some of the alternative arguments that the author neglected to include?

5. Draw your conclusion. Whether or not the argument is true, you can determine whether or not a good case was made. Did the author do a good job of supporting his or her main argument?

For Further Research

Kenneth L. Bakken, *The Journey into God: Healing and Christian Faith*. Minneapolis, MN: Augsburg Fortress Publishers, 2000.

Stephen Barrett, "Some Thoughts About Faith Healing." Quackwatch.org, 2003. Online. Available: http://www.quackwatch.org/01QuackeryRelatedTopics/faith.html.

Stephen Barrett and William T. Jarvis, eds., *The Health Robbers: A Close Look at Quackery in America*. Buffalo, NY: Prometheus Books, 1993.

Matthew Barry, "Adventures in Faith Healing." *Freethought Today*, March 1998. Online. Available: http://www.ffrf.org/fttoday/1998/march98/barry.html.

Richard J. Brenneman, *Deadly Blessings: Faith Healing on Trial*. Buffalo, NY: Prometheus Books, 1990.

Kurt Butler, *A Consumer's Guide to "Alternative Medicine": A Close Look at Homeopathy, Acupuncture, Faith-Healing, and Other Unconventional Treatments*. Buffalo, NY: Prometheus Books, 1992.

Norman Cousins, *Anatomy of an Illness As Perceived by the Patient: Reflections on Healing and Regeneration*. New York: W.W. Norton & Company, 2005.

Thomas Csordas, *Body/Meaning/Healing*. New York: Palgrave Macmillan, 2002.

Vinton A. Dearing, *The Great Physician*. Philadelphia: Xlibris Corporation, 2001.

Sue C. DeLaune and Patricia K. Ladner, *Fundamentals of Nursing: Standards and Practices*. Clifton Park, NY: Thomson Delmar Learning, 2002.

Jeff Doles, *Healing Scriptures and Prayers*. Seffner, FL: Walking Barefoot Ministries, 2003.

"Faith Healing." ApologeticsIndex.org. Online. Available: http://www.apologeticsindex.org/f06.html.

"Faith Healing." Infidels.org. Online. Available: http://www.infidels.org/library/modern/paranormal/healing.html

Bruce L. Flamm, "Faith Healing Confronts Modern Medicine." *The Scientific Review of Alternative Medicine*. Vol. 8, No. 1: 9–13, 2004.

Marc Galanter, *Cults: Faith, Healing and Coercion*. New York: Oxford University Press, 1999.

R.A. Hughes, "Psychological Perspectives on Infanticide in a Faith Healing Sect." *Pyschotherapy*, 27: 107–115, 1990.

Daniel Hurley, *Facing Pain, Finding Hope: A Physician Examines Pain, Faith, and the Healing Stories of Jesus*. Chicago: Loyola Press, 2005.

Stephen Jackson, *"Foul Demons, Come Out!": The Rhetoric of Twentieth-Century American Faith Healing*. Westport, CT: Praeger Publishers, 1999.

Philip Jenkins, *Mystics and Messiahs: Cults and New Religions in American History*. New York: Oxford University Press, 2000.

Ari Kiev, ed., *Magic, Faith, and Healing: Studies in Primitive Psychiatry*. Lanham, MD: Jason Aronson, Publisher, 1996.

Dana E. King, *Faith, Spirituality, and Medicine: Toward the Making of the Healing Practitioner*. Binghamton, NY: The Haworth Press, 2000.

Harold Koenig, *Spirituality in Patient Care: Why, How, When, and What*. Templeton, PA: Templeton Foundation Press, 2002.

Jean Maalouf, *The Healing Power of Faith (Healing Power)*. Mystic, CT: Twenty-Third Publications, 2004.

George M. Marsden, *Understanding Fundamentalism and Evangelicalism*. Grand Rapids, MI: Wm. B. Eerdmans Publishing Co., 1991.

Sarah M. Pike, *New Age and Neopagan Religions in America*. New York: Columbia University Press, 2004.

Alison Dundes Renteln, *The Cultural Defense*. New York: Oxford University Press, 2004.

Ailon Shiloh, *Faith Healing: The Religious Experience as a Therapeutic Process*. Springfield, IL: Charles C. Thomas, Publisher, 1981.

Andrew Weil, *Health and Healing*. Boston: Houghton Mifflin, 1998.

Roanne Weisman, *Own Your Health: Choosing the Best from Alternative & Conventional Medicine: Experts to Guide You, Research to Inform You, Stories to Inspire You*. Deerfield Beach, FL: Health Communications, Inc., 2003.

Index

DELTA COLLEGE LIBRARY

3 1434 00341 4517

DISCARD

MAR 12 2013 ✓

BT 732.5 .F35 2006

Faith healing
9/2010